CONFIDENCE MINDSET IN 30 DAYS

30 DAYS TO ALIGNMENT SERIES
BOOK 4

IMANI BLAKE

30 DAYS TO ALIGNMENT SERIES
IMANI BLAKE

CONFIDENCE MINDSET IN 30 DAYS

Shift How You Think, Speak, And Show Up In Your Real Life

Oshun Publications

Confidence Mindset in 30 Days © Copyright 2025 Imani Blake

ISBN 978-1-961362-63-5 (Paperback)

ISBN 978-1-961362-64-2 (Hardback)

ISBN 978-1-961362-62-8 (eBook)

All rights reserved

The content contained within this book may not be reproduced, duplicated or transmitted without direct written permission from the author or the publisher.

Under no circumstances will any blame or legal responsibility be held against the publisher, or author, for any damages, reparation, or monetary loss due to the information contained within this book, either directly or indirectly.

Legal Notice

This book is copyright protected. It is only for personal use. You cannot amend, distribute, sell, use, quote or paraphrase any part, or the content within this book, without the consent of the author or publisher.

Disclaimer Notice

Please note the information contained within this document is for educational and entertainment purposes only. All effort has been executed to present accurate, up to date, reliable, complete information. No warranties of any kind are declared or implied. Readers acknowledge that the author is not engaged in the rendering of legal, financial, medical or professional advice. The content within this book has been derived from various sources. Please consult a licensed professional before attempting any techniques outlined in this book.

By reading this document, the reader agrees that under no circumstances is the author responsible for any losses, direct or indirect, that are incurred as a result of the use of the information contained within this document, including, but not limited to, errors, omissions, or inaccuracies.

Book Cover Design by Inkspire Designs

Published by Oshun Publications

9 Old Kings Road Suite 123 #1038; Palm Coast, FL 32137

www.oshunpublications.com

30 DAYS TO ALIGNMENT SERIES

Abundance Mindset in 30 Days
Money Mindset in 30 Days
Manifestation for Beginners in 30 Days
Confidence Mindset in 30 Days
Love Mindset in 30 Days
Wealth Habits in 30 Days
Magnetic Energy in 30 Days
Spiritual Success in 30 Days

CONTENTS

Introduction: Confidence Is Something You Build	ix
Week 1: Shift How You Think	1
Day 1: Redefining Confidence for Real Life	5
Day 2: Where Self-Doubt Begins	11
Day 3: Spotting Thoughts That Aren't Yours	17
Day 4: Perfection vs. Progress	23
Day 5: Fear of Judgment	29
Day 6: The Trap of Playing Small	35
Day 7: Building Self-Respect Through Awareness	41
Week 2: Shift How You Speak	47
Day 8: Listening to Your Inner Voice	51
Day 9: Replace Criticism With Honesty	57
Day 10: Choosing Neutral Over Negative	63
Day 11: Speaking to Yourself With Trust	69
Day 12: Reframing "I Can't" and "I'm Not"	75
Day 13: Stop Calling Yourself "Too Much" or "Not Enough"	81
Day 14: Quiet Strength in Everyday Speech	87
Week 3: Shift How You Show Up	93
Day 15: Say What You Mean	95
Day 16: Make One Bold Ask	99
Day 17: Hold Your Ground in Small Moments	105
Day 18: Speaking With Steady Pace and Clarity	111
Day 19: Walking Into Spaces Like You Belong	117
Day 20: The Confidence of Saying No	123
Day 21: Stop Over-Apologizing	129
Week 4: Keep Showing Up for Yourself	135
Day 22: Let Go of Impressing Others	137
Day 23: Finding Safety Without Hiding	141
Day 24: The Power of "I Don't Know Yet"	145
Day 25: Keeping Promises to Yourself	151

Day 26: Feeling Confident vs. Looking Confident	157
Day 27: Confidence Is Practice, Not Perfection	163
Day 28: Collecting Your Wins as Evidence	169
Day 29: You Don't Need Permission to Be Worthy	175
Day 30: Becoming Who You Already Are	181
30 Days of Confidence Journal Prompts	187
15 Quick Scripts for Boundaries, Asking, and Speaking Up	195
Closing Reflection: Keep Building, Keep Showing Up	199
Bibliography	203
Newsletter Signup	205
About the Author	207

INTRODUCTION: CONFIDENCE IS SOMETHING YOU BUILD

When people discuss confidence, the image that often comes to mind is that of someone bold, loud, or always knowing what to say. This might be the student who eagerly raises their hand to answer every question in class or the person who confidently enters a room and seems to know everyone. However, it's crucial to understand that confidence isn't about being outgoing, loud, or perfect. It's not an innate trait or something only a select few possess.

Confidence is a mindset. It's how you think about yourself. It's something you can grow one day at a time.

Even if you're feeling nervous, even if your voice shakes, even if you've been quiet your whole life, you can build confidence. This book is here to guide you through this gradual process.

What Is a Confidence Mindset?

Confidence isn't about thinking you're better than everyone else. It's not about being fearless, either. Real confidence means trusting that you are allowed to be yourself. It means believing your thoughts matter. It means showing up even when you're unsure.

A confident mindset is the way you choose to think about yourself every day. It doesn't mean you'll never feel doubt again. It means you learn to notice the doubt and keep going anyway.

You don't need to change who you are to be confident. You just need to change the way you treat yourself in your own mind.

Confidence Comes From What You Think, Say, and Do

Confidence shows up in small ways all the time. It's in the thoughts you choose to believe. It's in the way you talk to yourself. It's in your choices, even the tiny ones.

For example:

- When you say, "I can try," instead of "I'll mess it up," you're choosing a confidence mindset.
- When you tell someone what you need, even if it feels awkward, you're building trust with yourself.
- When you stop saying "sorry" for things that don't need an apology, you're letting yourself take up space.

Your thoughts shape how you feel. Your words shape how you show up. Your actions shape what you believe is possible. Confidence doesn't come all at once. It's built with small steps. You already have some confidence inside you. This book will help you recognize it, cultivate it, and apply it in your daily life.

How This 30-Day Guide Works

This guide is set up to help you build confidence slowly and steadily. Each day, you'll read a short lesson and then reflect on its meaning for you. You'll be asked to try small practices, each lasting 5 to 10 minutes. They aren't hard. They're designed to help you notice your thoughts, speak kindly to yourself, and act with more self-trust.

Here's what you'll find each day:

- A simple message about confidence
- A real-life example or story to show how it works
- A daily thought or phrase to repeat to yourself
- A short reflection or writing activity
- A small practice or challenge for the day

Some days will feel easy. Others might feel harder. Both are okay. This isn't about doing things perfectly. It's about showing up each day, even if all you can give is one quiet moment of attention to yourself.

You don't have to finish every page in order or on a tight schedule. However, the more often you return, the more your mindset will shift. This guide is here to walk with you, not rush you.

What You'll Need

You don't need anything fancy to get started. But here are a few things that may help:

- A notebook or journal to write down your daily reflections
- A quiet spot where you can read and think
- A little bit of time each day (even just 10 minutes)

Try not to skip the reflection parts. Writing things down helps your brain remember what matters. Even if you just write a sentence or two, it will help you connect more deeply with yourself.

Your Confidence Intention

Before you begin, let's pause and set a personal intention. An intention is a simple sentence about how you want to grow or what you hope to learn.

This isn't a big goal like "I want to be fearless by next month." Instead, it's a quiet promise you make to yourself. Something like:

- "I want to be kinder to myself."
- "I want to stop hiding so much."
- "I want to speak up more, even if I feel nervous."
- "I want to trust my voice."

Take a moment and write your own. There's no wrong answer. Just think about why you picked up this book. What are you hoping for?

Here's space for you to write your intention:

My Confidence Intention:

Now, look at that sentence. Reread it. This is your starting place. Whenever you feel stuck, return to this thought. This is what you're building toward, not someone else's version of confidence, but your own.

A Note Before You Begin

Some days, this work will feel exciting. You'll try something new, say what you really think, or make a choice that feels strong.

Other days, it might feel like you're going backward. You might slip into old habits. You might doubt yourself again. That's okay.

Confidence is not a straight line. It's more like a winding path with small wins and quiet moments of courage. What matters most is that you keep showing up.

You're not behind. You're not broken. You don't need to fix who you are. You're just learning to stand with yourself, one step at a time.

This book isn't asking you to be someone else. It's asking you to stop hiding the person you already are.

Let's Begin

You're here because you're ready to grow. Not because you need to be perfect, but because you want to treat yourself with more trust and care.

Every word in this guide is here to remind you: You are already enough. You can build trust in yourself. You can speak more clearly. You can show up without shrinking.

One day. One thought. One small act of confidence at a time.

Let's begin.

WEEK 1: SHIFT HOW YOU THINK

THEME: ***Rewiring thoughts that fuel self-doubt***

Confidence doesn't begin with what people see on the outside. It starts in your thoughts those quiet sentences that run through your mind all day long. Some of these thoughts push you forward. But many hold you back. This week is about starting where confidence really begins: in your own mind.

Self-doubt doesn't come out of nowhere. It grows from repeated thoughts that say things like, *"I'm not good enough,"* *"What if I fail?"* or *"I should be more like them."* You might not even realize you're thinking these things because they've been around for so long. Maybe you heard them from someone else. Maybe they helped you feel safer in the past. But now, they're getting in the way.

This week, your goal is not to force yourself to be positive all the time. It's about being more honest about the way you speak to yourself and practicing more helpful ways of thinking. For instance, instead of 'I'm not good enough,' you could say 'I am enough and I am constantly improving.' you'll begin to notice when a thought is based on fear or habit, not truth. You'll start to choose thoughts that are more grounded, kinder, and more genuine.

This isn't about pretending everything is perfect. It's about learning how to stay with yourself even when things feel messy. Your mind has been trained to believe certain stories about you. But you're allowed to question those stories. You're allowed to say, *"That's not true anymore."*

This week, you'll embark on a journey of self-discovery, exploring the origins of self-doubt. You'll learn to recognize thoughts that were passed on to you by others thoughts that don't actually belong to you. You'll delve into the difference between striving for perfection, which often leads to self-doubt, and making genuine progress, which is about learning and growing. You'll confront the fear of being judged and learn how to keep going anyway. You'll also notice where you've been playing small not because you aren't capable, but because you were taught to shrink.

The goal isn't to fix yourself. You're not broken. The goal is to get more aware. With awareness, you can start making better choices ones that are based on truth, not fear.

Each day will give you one clear idea to focus on, along with a short reflection and a simple action you can try. Some of it may be challenging. That's okay. New thoughts take time to stick. But the more you notice and name them, the easier it becomes to change them.

You're not trying to erase every doubt. You're on a journey to build trust in yourself, one thought at a time. This self-trust will serve as your anchor, guiding you through the process of reprogramming your thoughts and fueling your confidence.

Let's begin by taking control of the voice in your head. It has a lot to say. Now, you get to decide what you'll believe and what you're ready to leave behind. This is your journey, and you have the power to shape it.

DAY 1: REDEFINING CONFIDENCE FOR REAL LIFE

When most people think about confidence, they picture someone who walks into a room and owns it. Someone who is loud, outgoing, and full of energy. Maybe they imagine someone who never hesitates, always knows the right thing to say, and never feels nervous. But the truth is, absolute confidence doesn't have to look like that at all.

Confidence isn't about being loud. It isn't about always being sure or always getting it right. Confidence is something quieter, something steadier. It's how you treat yourself. It's how you keep going, even when you're unsure. And most of all, it's something you practice not something you either have or don't have.

Many people think confidence is a personality trait. They believe that some people are simply born confident, while others aren't. But confidence isn't about who you are it's about how you think, speak, and show up. It's a mindset, not a label. And that means it can be built. It can be learned. It can grow.

Confidence isn't one big thing you earn. It's something you build in small ways, every single day. It shows up when you speak honestly, when you keep trying after making a mistake, or when you let people see who you really are. Even when you're nervous. Even when your hands shake. Even when you're scared of being judged.

Sometimes, confidence looks like raising your hand in class even when you're not totally sure of the answer. Sometimes it's saying "no" when you're overwhelmed. Sometimes it's resting when your body is tired instead of pushing through just to please someone else. Confidence doesn't always look bold. Sometimes, it seems quiet. Still. Brave in its own soft way.

You've already shown confidence before even if you didn't call it that. Think back to the times you tried something new. The times you spoke up. The moments you kept going when something felt hard. Those weren't accidents. They were real moments of courage. That's what confidence really is: trusting yourself enough to try.

In this 30-day guide, you'll practice building a more honest kind of confidence. You'll stop trying to be perfect and start showing up as yourself. You'll learn to notice old habits of thinking especially the ones that tell you you're not good enough. And you'll begin to speak to yourself with more trust and respect.

You won't need to change your whole personality. You won't need to "fake it till you make it." You'll just need to show up, day by day, and try something new even in small ways. This process isn't about becoming someone else. It's about becoming more yourself.

Let's start by letting go of the old picture of confidence the one that says you have to be fearless, perfect, or always "on." That version leaves many people out. And it puts way too much pressure on everyone.

Instead, let's try a new picture of confidence. A real one.

Confidence is:

- Saying what you really think, even if your voice is soft.
- Showing up when something matters to you.
- Owning your needs without apology.
- Admitting when you don't know something and being open to learn.
- Trying again after something didn't go well.
- Letting yourself be seen not the perfect version, but the real one.

Confidence also means being kind to yourself on the days when things don't go the way you hoped. It means not beating yourself up for feeling nervous, awkward, or unsure. It means trusting that you are still growing, still learning, and still allowed to take up space.

When you stop trying to look confident and start focusing on being honest, things begin to change. You don't have to pretend anymore. You don't have to perform. You just start being more yourself and believing that who you are is enough.

This shift might feel uncomfortable at first. That's normal. You've been told a lot of things about who you should be. You've been trained to think confidence means being the best, looking a certain way, or never making mistakes. But you're allowed to question that. You're allowed to rewrite what confidence means for you.

Over the next 30 days, you'll have simple lessons and daily practices that are designed to be achievable, helping you build your confidence in fundamental, doable ways. Some days will feel easy. Some might feel hard. That's okay. You don't have to get it perfect. You just have to keep showing up.

Each day, you'll reflect on your thoughts, practice using your voice, and take small actions that help build trust with yourself. This process of self-reflection is where real confidence comes from: not from other people's praise, but from your own consistent effort and care.

Today's small step is about setting your intention. Take a moment to ask yourself: What do I want to get out of these next 30 days? There's no correct answer. What matters is that it's honest and meaningful to you. This is your journey, and you are in control.

Maybe you want to:

- Speak up more often.
- Stop overthinking everything.
- Be kinder to yourself.
- Stop shrinking to make others comfortable.
- Ask for what you need without guilt.
- Let go of trying to be perfect.

There's no correct answer. What matters is that it's honest and meaningful to you.

Once you have your intention, write it down somewhere you'll see it every day. This is your reminder your anchor. You're not doing this to impress anyone. You're doing it to build something real and lasting inside yourself.

Confidence doesn't show up all at once. It grows with each small step, each honest word, and each time you choose to try instead of hide. And the more you practice, the more natural it becomes.

So today, start with this thought:

Confidence is not about being someone else. It's about showing up as me and trusting that's enough.

You don't have to rush. You don't have to prove anything. You just have to begin.

Let today be the day you stop waiting for confidence to arrive and start building it, one step at a time.

DAY 2: WHERE SELF-DOUBT BEGINS

SELF-DOUBT IS NOT AN ABRUPT VISITOR. It's a slow builder, often sneaking in without your conscious awareness. It starts with seemingly insignificant triggers a comment, a glance, a moment that made you question your worth. These moments accumulate over time, shaping your self-perception if left unaddressed.

Reflect on your childhood. You probably didn't worry too much about what others thought. You played, explored, asked questions, and tried things just to see what would happen. If you fell down, you got back up. You weren't afraid of being seen. You didn't overthink your words. You just were.

But somewhere along the way, things shifted.

Maybe someone told you to "stop showing off" when you were excited. Maybe you were laughed at when you gave the wrong answer in class. Maybe someone told you your dreams were too big or that you weren't good enough. Even if they didn't mean to hurt you, those moments leave marks. And your brain always trying to keep you safe takes note.

Your brain's primary function is to shield you from danger, including emotional threats. When you experience embarrassment, rejection, or criticism, your brain takes note and urges you to avoid similar situations. This is how self-doubt forms, as a protective mechanism. But over time, this protection can feel like a confinement, hindering you from expressing yourself, trying new things, or revealing your true self.

Remember, self-doubt is not a sign of weakness. It's a common human experience.

There are lots of places self-doubt can begin. For many people, it starts at home. You may have been raised by adults who were doing their best but didn't know how to support your confidence. Maybe they thought being strict would help you succeed. Maybe they were dealing with their own insecurities. Perhaps they simply didn't understand how their words came across.

If you were told things like "Be realistic," "Don't get your hopes up," or "That's not for people like us," you may have started to believe you shouldn't aim too high. Or maybe your feelings were brushed off with comments like "Don't be so sensitive" or "Toughen up." Those words might seem minor at the time, but they add up. They teach you to doubt your instincts and to question your worth.

School is another place where self-doubt often grows. You might remember moments when you raised your hand and got the answer wrong. Or when a teacher made you feel like your effort wasn't enough. Maybe you were picked last for a team or teased for something you wore. Even one painful moment like that can be enough to make you want to shrink, stay quiet, or hide who you are.

Then there's the world around us friends, media, social rules. Maybe a friend made fun of your idea. Maybe you tried to speak up, and someone told you to be quiet. Maybe you saw a certain "perfect" image online or on TV and felt like you could never match it. Over time, you start to wonder, "Am I too much?" or "Am I not enough?"

The worst part? These thoughts start to sound like your own voice. But they're not. They were picked up from the outside from people, places, and systems that made you feel small. And once you've heard them enough times, your brain plays them back like a recording: "You're not ready. You'll probably fail. Don't bother."

The truth is, these thoughts aren't facts. They're habits. And the good news? Habits can be changed.

You don't have to believe every thought that pops into your head. Especially the ones that say you can't, you shouldn't, or you're not enough. That voice of doubt isn't the real you it's a collection of old lessons that no longer serve you.

Today is about becoming more aware of where those lessons came from.

Start by thinking about one moment in your past that made you shrink. Someone may have corrected you in front of others. You were told to tone it down or not take up too much space. Your best effort was ignored or criticized. Take a minute to really remember that moment.

Now ask yourself: Was that moment truly about you? Or was it about someone else's fear, frustration, or misunderstanding?

Often, the person who made you feel small wasn't trying to be cruel. They were passing along their own self-doubt. They had their own story of being judged or silenced. And even though it affected you, it didn't start with you.

That doesn't make it okay. But it does help you understand that your self-doubt isn't a personal flaw. It's a learned response. And once you see that, you can start to choose differently.

So what can you do when that voice of self-doubt shows up?

The first step is to notice it. Pay attention to when it shows up and what it says. Does it sound like someone from your past? Does it use the exact words you've heard before?

The next step is to separate yourself from it. Instead of saying "I'm not good at this," try saying, "This is a thought I'm having, not a truth." That one slight shift gives you space. Space to question the thought instead of just accepting it.

You can also replace that voice with something kinder and more honest. You don't have to go from "I can't" to "I'm amazing." That might feel fake. But you can go from "I can't" to "I'm learning." Or from "I'm not good at this" to "I'm doing my best right now."

Over time, these new thoughts will become stronger. And the old ones? They'll get quieter.

You don't need to erase every self-doubt in one day. That's not the goal. The goal is to start seeing where those doubts came from and to stop letting them run the show.

Confidence isn't the absence of self-doubt. It's the choice to keep showing up anyway.

So today, take a moment to tell yourself: "I'm not broken. I've just been taught to question myself. And I can learn something new."

This is your reminder that confidence can be built. You're already doing it.

Keep going.

DAY 3: SPOTTING THOUGHTS THAT AREN'T YOURS

SOME THOUGHTS DON'T REALLY BELONG to you, but they live in your head anyway.

It may initially sound peculiar, but not all thoughts in your brain are your own. Many of the thoughts we carry were not born within us. They were inherited, taught, repeated, or absorbed over time like background noise that became part of our internal voice.

Some of those thoughts are helpful. They guide us. They remind us of what matters. But others? They tear us down, limit us, or stop us from speaking up. And often, those aren't our thoughts at all. They're someone else's opinions, fears, or judgments that got stuck in our minds and started repeating like they were true.

Today's goal is to not just notice those thoughts, but to take back control. To see them clearly and confidently declare, "Wait a second that isn't mine." This is the first step towards reclaiming your mental space and building your confidence.

Let's take an example.

Say you're about to raise your hand in class or speak up in a group. And suddenly a voice in your head says: "Don't do that. You'll sound stupid." You pause. You shrink back. And the moment passes.

That voice might feel like your own, but it probably isn't.

Maybe a teacher once scolded you for giving the wrong answer. Maybe someone laughed at you when you mispronounced a word. Maybe you've seen others get shut down for trying something bold. Over time, those moments leave marks. And your brain trying to protect you from more discomfort plays back those experiences in the form of self-doubt.

But here's the thing: that voice isn't speaking the truth. It's just repeating an old warning. A warning you didn't ask for and no longer need.

This happens in all kinds of ways. You might hear thoughts like:

- "I'm not good enough."
- "I should know better."
- "People like me don't do that."
- "I always mess things up."
- "They'll never take me seriously."

Ask yourself: where did that come from?

Think about how many voices you've been exposed to over the years parents, teachers, classmates, media, strangers, even social media comments. Every day, people share their opinions about what's right, smart, acceptable, pretty, or strong. And if you're not careful, you start to believe that what they say is true about you.

But just because someone said it doesn't make it true.

Let's say you were told as a kid that you were "too loud" or "too dramatic." Maybe it happened once, or maybe it happened a lot. You might have started believing that your personality was a problem. So now, as an adult or teen, when you get excited or passionate, you pull back. You tone yourself down. You apologize for being expressive. But was there ever really anything wrong with your excitement? Or did someone just feel uncomfortable with your joy?

Here's another one: maybe you were quiet and thoughtful growing up and someone told you to "speak up more" or accused you of being "too shy." So you started believing you weren't confident or that being quiet meant you were less. Again, the issue wasn't you. It was someone else's discomfort with silence.

These are examples of how someone else's opinion can sneak into your inner voice.

And it happens a lot.

This is why learning to spot these thoughts is such a big part of building confidence. Because as long as you're carrying around other people's judgments, you won't feel safe being yourself. You'll continue to try to shape yourself to fit what someone else once said you "should" be.

So how do you tell which thoughts are really yours?

Start by asking questions.

When a negative thought pops up, pause and ask:

- "Did I choose this thought, or did I inherit it?"
- "Whose voice does this sound like?"
- "Is this thought helping me, or holding me back?"
- "Would I say this to someone I care about?"

Remember, you don't need perfect answers. You just need curiosity. The act of asking these questions gives you distance from the thought. It helps you see that not everything in your head is the truth. Some of it is just old noise. And that realization can bring a sense of relief and freedom.

And here's the most important part: you're allowed to let go of thoughts that don't serve you. You don't have to keep replaying a judgment just because it's familiar. You don't have to keep believing something just because you've thought it a hundred times.

Remember, you have the power to rewrite your internal script. You don't have to keep replaying a judgment just because it's familiar. You don't have to keep believing something just because you've thought it a hundred times.

Let's practice that.

Take a common self-doubting thought, like: "I'm bad at this."

Instead of taking that thought at face value, stop and ask:

- "Where did I learn to think that?"
- "Who told me that?"
- "Was it true then? Is it true now?"
- "What would I say to a friend who felt this way?"

Then try replacing that thought with something more honest and helpful. Not fake. Just a small shift. Like:

- "I'm still learning this."
- "It's okay to not get it perfect."
- "This is something I'm working on."
- "One moment doesn't define my ability."

These new thoughts may feel awkward at first. That's normal. They're new. You're not trying to force confidence you're trying to be fair to yourself. And fairness is the foundation of self-respect.

Another way to spot thoughts that aren't yours is to notice when you say or think words like:

- "I should…"
- "I have to…"
- "They'll think…"

Those are often signs that a belief is being driven by pressure or fear, not truth. For example:

- "I should be more outgoing." (Says who?)
- "I have to be perfect or I'll look bad." (Where did that rule come from?)
- "They'll think I'm weird if I try that." (Who exactly is 'they'? And do you even agree with them?)

The truth is, the people who judge you harshly are often dealing with their own fears. Their opinions say more about their own mindset than about your worth.

Your job isn't to silence every doubtful thought. That's impossible. Your job is to know which ones are yours and which ones you can release.

You'll still have insecure moments. Everyone does. But now, when those thoughts show up, you can look at them with more awareness. You can ask questions, take a breath, and choose whether to believe them.

Confidence begins when you stop treating every thought like a fact.

So today, pay attention to your inner voice. When something makes you feel small, ask where it came from. If it didn't start with you, it doesn't need to stay with you.

You're allowed to think differently now.

You're allowed to choose thoughts that make room for who you really are.

And you're allowed to keep going, even when the old noise tries to return.

This is how confidence grows one thought at a time.

DAY 4: PERFECTION VS. PROGRESS

MOST PEOPLE THINK they have to be perfect before they try something. They want to get everything right. They don't want to fail, make a mistake, or feel embarrassed. So they wait. And wait. And wait.

But while they're waiting to be perfect, life keeps going.

Here's the truth: you don't need to be perfect. You just need to start.

Confidence doesn't come from being flawless. It comes from moving forward, even when you're unsure. It grows every time you try something, learn from it, and try again. That's what progress looks like.

Perfection is a heavy weight. It makes you feel like nothing is ever good enough. It keeps you stuck because you're afraid to get it wrong. But getting things wrong is how we learn. That's how we grow. And confidence grows with it.

Let's examine what perfection entails.

Perfection tells you:

- "You need to do this exactly right or don't do it at all."
- "You're not ready yet."
- "If you mess up, everyone will notice."
- "You should wait until you're sure."

These thoughts might sound helpful, but they're actually full of fear. They don't help you improve. They just make you afraid to begin.

Now, let's look at progress.

Progress says:

- "It's okay to start small."
- "Mistakes help me learn."
- "Trying is better than staying stuck."
- "Done is better than perfect."

Progress doesn't expect you to know everything. It just asks you to take the next step. Then the next. And then the next one after that.

Think of a baby learning to walk. Do we expect babies to take perfect steps right away? No. We cheer when they fall down and get back up. That's how learning works. That's what progress is.

But as we get older, we start to think we have to get it right the first time. We forget that we're allowed to grow.

Sometimes, people avoid trying new things because they think others will judge them. They think, "If I'm not the best, I'll look silly." Or, "If I don't have it all figured out, I should stay quiet." But those thoughts come from fear, not truth.

Everyone starts somewhere. No one begins as an expert. Every strong speaker, confident leader, or skilled artist you know? They all started with small, messy first steps. The only difference is that they kept going.

Perfection wants you to look good. Progress wants you to get better.

Perfection tries to impress others. Progress is about doing your best for yourself.

Perfection is about being seen a certain way. Progress is about showing up as you are.

Let's say you want to try something new, such as raising your hand in class, applying for a job, speaking in front of people, or starting a creative project. Perfection might tell you to wait until you're "ready." But how do you get ready without trying?

You don't.

You get ready by doing the thing. That's how absolute confidence is built.

Let's look at a few examples.

Imagine Maya wants to start writing, but she keeps deleting her work. She thinks it has to sound perfect before she can share it. Every time she writes, she criticizes herself and gives up. So she never finishes anything. That's perfection holding her back.

Now, imagine Maya shifts her thinking. She says, "I'm going to write for 10 minutes. I don't care if it's messy." She writes a short piece. It's not perfect, but she keeps going. Each day, she writes a little more. Soon, she's more confident. She starts to enjoy the process. That's progress.

Now imagine Jordan wants to share an idea in a meeting. He's quiet most of the time because he thinks, "What if I say the wrong thing?" That thought keeps him silent.

But one day, he says something simple. It's not perfect. His voice shakes a little. But afterward, someone says, "Thanks for sharing that." Jordan feels proud. That small moment of courage helped him grow. That's progress.

Progress isn't flashy. It's not always exciting. But it adds up. Little by little, it builds something strong. Every try counts. This is where determination comes in, pushing you to keep going, even when the path seems unclear.

Here's the thing: perfection is a moving target. Even if you think you've reached it, your brain will often say, "You could've done better." That's why chasing perfection never feels finished. You never feel good enough, because the rules keep changing.

Progress is different. Progress says, "Hey, I did something I couldn't do last week. That's worth something." And it is.

If you wait for perfection, you might wait forever. But if you choose progress, you can start now. It's a liberating feeling, knowing that you don't have to be perfect to begin your journey.

Let's make this shift real today.

When you catch yourself saying, "This has to be perfect," pause and ask:

- "Is this thought helping me or stopping me?"
- "What's one small step I can take right now?"
- "Can I be proud of trying, even if it's not perfect?"

Write down a moment from your past when you were proud not because you did something perfectly, but because you showed up and tried. That's real confidence. That's the kind you want to grow.

Now, think of something you've been putting off because you want to get it just right. What would happen if you gave yourself permission to do it halfway? To be messy? To figure it out while you do it?

That's what progress feels like. And it's more powerful than perfection ever will be.

Try saying this to yourself today:

"Progress over perfect. I'd rather try than wait."

Repeat it when your brain says, "You're not ready."

Repeat it when fear shows up.

Repeat it when you're tempted to quit before you even begin.

You are allowed to learn. You are allowed to grow out loud. You don't have to wait until everything looks polished to take a step forward.

Perfection might feel safe, but it keeps you small. Progress feels brave even when it's quiet and unsure.

So today, take the step. Even a small one. Even if it's wobbly.

You don't need to be perfect. You just need to begin.

DAY 5: FEAR OF JUDGMENT

HAVE you ever stopped yourself from doing something not because you couldn't do it but because you were scared of what someone else might think? Maybe you wanted to raise your hand in class to ask a question, wear a unique outfit to a social event, share an innovative idea in a group discussion, or try a new hobby, but a little voice in your head said, "What if they laugh?" or "What if I look stupid?"

That feeling, the fear of judgment, is not unique to you. It's a common experience, one that almost everyone feels at some point.

Fear of judgment is the worry that other people might not like what you say, what you wear, what you do, or who you are. It's that uncomfortable feeling that says, "They're watching me," even when they're not. It's the part of you that wants to stay quiet or invisible just to feel safe.

This fear often starts early. Maybe someone laughed at you when you made a mistake. Perhaps you were told to "be quiet," "don't be so dramatic," or "stop trying so hard." Maybe you once shared something that felt personal, and someone brushed it off or made fun of it. Those little moments stick. And before you even realize it, your brain decides that staying quiet, small, or hidden is safer than being seen.

But here's the thing: staying hidden doesn't protect your confidence. It holds it back.

You can't grow your confidence while hiding who you are.

You might tell yourself it's better not to be noticed. You might avoid raising your voice, sharing your work, or standing out. But what you're really doing is giving your power to other people's opinions, opinions that may not even be true or fair.

The truth is, people will always have opinions. Some will like what you do. Some won't. That's just how it works. But their opinions don't define you. And they don't have to stop you.

When you try to please everyone, you lose yourself. You start making choices based on what others *might* think, rather than what *you* want. You water yourself down. You second-guess. You hold back. And slowly, you start to forget how powerful your own voice really is.

The most confident people aren't the ones who never get judged. They're the ones who make a conscious decision to stop letting fear of judgment dictate their choices. They speak up, they wear what they like, they ask questions, they try new things. Not because they know everyone will cheer, but because they've realized that their voice matters more than other people's opinions.

They speak up even when it's scary. They wear what they like. They ask questions. They try new things. Not because they know everyone will cheer, but because they've decided their voice matters more than other people's opinions.

This takes practice. And courage. But it's something you can build one small moment at a time.

Let's talk about what fear of judgment *sounds* like. These thoughts might show up in your head:

- "They'll think I'm weird."
- "I don't want to sound dumb."
- "Who am I to do that?"
- "People are going to judge me."
- "It's safer if I just stay quiet."

These thoughts can feel true, but they're often just old fears replaying themselves. The brain tries to keep you safe by avoiding risk. But speaking your truth, trying something new, or showing up as yourself is not a danger. It's growth.

Instead of letting those thoughts run the show, you can start asking different questions:

- "What if I'm proud of myself for trying?"
- "What if my voice helps someone else?"
- "What if being seen is how I grow?"

Not everyone will understand you. That's okay. Confidence doesn't mean everyone agrees with you. It means you agree with *yourself*. It means you like who you are and what you stand for. It means showing up even when it's not perfect or popular.

Confidence isn't about being fearless. It's about acknowledging your fear and showing up anyway. It's about feeling scared and doing it anyway. That's the true essence of confidence.

You don't need to be loud to be bold. You don't need to be perfect to be proud. You don't need everyone to clap for you to know that your work matters.

Your job is not to make everyone comfortable. Your job is to tell the truth about who you are.

Let's be honest: sometimes, people will judge. Sometimes, they'll whisper or roll their eyes. But that says more about them than it does about you.

People judge when they feel small inside. They judge when they're afraid to be themselves. If someone laughs at your effort, it's because they haven't found the strength to try themselves.

So let them watch. Let them whisper. And keep going.

Because every time you choose to show up instead of shut down, you get a little braver.

Every time you speak up, even when your voice shakes, you're practicing confidence.

Every time you say, "This is who I am," even when others don't get it, you're growing stronger.

Here's something simple you can practice today: let yourself be seen.

That might mean speaking your mind in a group. Wearing the thing you actually love. Sharing your work, even if it's not perfect. Or just not apologizing for being different.

Start with one small thing. Don't wait until the fear is gone. Do it even with the fear sitting beside you.

And when that fear whispers, "What if they judge you?" answer back: "Let them. I'm not doing this for them. I'm doing it for me."

Try saying this to yourself today:

"I don't need everyone to understand me. I'm proud of who I am."

Confidence is not about never feeling fear. It's about not letting fear control your life.

You've already been judged before. You've already felt unsure. And you've survived it. So now you get to choose: will you keep shrinking for people who don't see your worth, or will you start showing up for yourself?

You have something to say. Something to create. Something to offer. Don't keep it hidden just because someone *might* not like it.

You don't need everyone to agree. You just need to trust that you're allowed to be here, just as you are.

Let's keep showing up.

One thought at a time.

One step at a time.

One brave moment at a time.

You've got this.

DAY 6: THE TRAP OF PLAYING SMALL

HAVE you ever held yourself back not because you weren't capable, but because you didn't want to stand out? Maybe you didn't raise your hand, even though you knew the answer. Maybe you kept your ideas to yourself because you thought people might not take you seriously. Maybe you said, "It's fine," even when it wasn't. That's what playing small looks like. And most of us do it more often than we realize.

Playing small isn't always about being quiet or shy; it's about being cautious. It's about shrinking yourself to feel safe. It's pretending you don't care when you do. It's staying silent when you want to speak. It's hiding your talent because you're afraid someone might judge it. It's saying "I'm not ready" over and over, even when part of you knows you are.

Sometimes playing small sounds polite. Sometimes it looks like being easygoing. You tell yourself, "It's not a big deal," or "I don't want to be too much," or "I'll just wait until later." But deep down, there's a cost. When you keep pushing yourself down, you start to believe that's where you belong.

The world may have taught you to stay small. Maybe someone told you not to brag, not to make a fuss, not to get ahead of yourself. Maybe you learned early that it's safer to be agreeable than honest. Perhaps you were once laughed at for trying. And so you pulled back.

But let's be clear about one thing: playing small is not humility. It's not grace. It's not easy to work with. It's fear in disguise.

When you play small, you trade your truth for comfort. You choose safety over growth. You avoid risk, but you also avoid your own potential.

Let's talk about what playing small can look like in real life. Maybe you lower your prices or don't ask for what you're worth because you're scared of hearing no. Maybe you don't speak up in meetings, even though you have ideas. Maybe you don't ask for help when you need it because you don't want to bother anyone. Maybe you don't tell people what you really want because you think it's "too much."

You might brush off compliments. You might say things like "It was nothing," or "It's not a big deal," even when it *was*. You might hold back your excitement, your creativity, your opinions just to avoid being "too much" for someone else.

And after a while, it becomes a habit. A quiet habit of hiding who you really are.

But here's the thing: confidence can't grow in the dark. It needs light. It needs air. It needs you to stop tucking yourself away and start showing up.

Confidence doesn't come from staying safe. It comes from taking small risks, little by little. It comes from standing in your truth even when it's uncomfortable. It comes from owning your voice even if it shakes.

Think about a time when you *didn't* play small. A time when you spoke up, took the lead, and shared something that mattered to you. How did it feel? Probably scary but also powerful. That's the thing about showing up fully: it stretches you. And even when it's scary, it builds trust in yourself.

Playing small may feel safer in the moment, but over time, it leaves you frustrated. You start to feel stuck, unseen, maybe even resentful. You begin to wonder why no one notices your work, why others seem more confident, and why it always feels like you're holding something back.

However, the truth is that people can't see what you're hiding.

If you want to be seen, heard, and respected, you have to stop hiding your light.

Now, this doesn't mean you need to shout to be heard. It doesn't mean you have to take over every room. Confidence doesn't mean being the loudest voice. It means being honest. It means showing up as *yourself* fully and freely.

Letting yourself take up space means you believe your presence matters. Your ideas matter. Your voice matters. And they do.

You don't have to be perfect to be seen. You don't have to be ready to be real. You just have to stop pretending that you're less than you are.

Today, start by noticing where you play small. Do you avoid sharing your wins? Do you pretend things don't bother you when they do? Do you let others lead, even when you have something to say?

You can start small. You don't need to change everything overnight. But every time you choose to speak up instead of staying quiet, you're breaking that old habit. Every time you stop apologizing for your needs, you're creating new patterns. Every time you share something real, you're building trust with yourself.

And it will feel uncomfortable at first. That's okay.

Growth often feels uncomfortable. But it's also freeing.

Here's something to say to yourself today:

"I don't have to shrink to fit into places I've outgrown."

You are allowed to want more. You are allowed to speak clearly. You are allowed to take pride in your work. You are allowed to ask for help, space, or whatever you need.

You don't need anyone's permission to stop playing small. You just need to decide that hiding isn't working for you anymore.

The people who are meant for you won't ask you to shrink. They'll make room for you to rise.

So today, stop shrinking.

Start sharing.

Let your voice be heard, not because you need to prove anything, but because you have something to say.

You don't have to be fearless to be brave.

You don't have to be loud to be strong.

You don't have to be perfect to be proud.

You just have to be real.

You've spent enough time dimming your light to make others comfortable.

Now, it's your time to shine, even if it feels awkward. Even if no one claps. Even if you're not sure you're ready.

You are ready.

Let yourself be seen.

Let yourself take up space.

Let yourself grow.

And don't play small, not today.

Not anymore.

DAY 7: BUILDING SELF-RESPECT THROUGH AWARENESS

CONFIDENCE DOESN'T START with doing something big. It begins with how you see yourself, moment by moment. A significant part of that is self-respect. When you respect yourself, you treat yourself with care. You trust your thoughts and your feelings. You stop talking down to yourself. You begin to believe that your voice matters.

But here's the thing: you can't build self-respect without the powerful tool of self-awareness. Take note of how you speak to yourself, how you behave when things become challenging, and where you might be neglecting your own needs. Today is about that kind of noticing. It's about waking up to how you treat yourself, not with blame, but with the empowering tools of kindness and curiosity.

Self-respect grows every time you show yourself that you matter. That your time, your energy, and your well-being are important. This doesn't mean being perfect or getting everything right. It means paying attention to what's really going on inside you, and nurturing yourself with self-compassion.

Awareness is where that begins.

Think about your day so far. How did you speak to yourself when you woke up? Did you take a moment to care for yourself, or did your thoughts immediately go to what you "should" do or what might go wrong?

When something small went wrong, perhaps you forgot something, spilled something, or made a mistake - what did your inner voice say? Did it help you move forward, or did it tear you down?

Most of us carry an inner voice that's been shaped by years of experiences, people's words, and old habits. That voice can be gentle and supportive. But more often, it's harsh. It might say things like:

- "Why did you do that?"
- "You always mess this up."
- "What's wrong with you?"

And the more we hear that voice, the more we start to believe it.

But that voice isn't *you*. It's a mix of past comments, fears, and doubts. And once you become aware of it, you can start to shift it.

Awareness is noticing without judgment. It's not about beating yourself up for being hard on yourself. It's about listening closely and asking, "Is this voice helping me or hurting me?" Then, slowly, you can begin to speak to yourself in a new way.

Here's how awareness builds self-respect:

You learn to pause.

Instead of reacting automatically, you take a breath and check in. You might ask, "What do I really need right now?" That simple pause can help you choose something that supports you, rather than something that tears you down.

You begin to hear the stories you tell yourself.

You start to notice patterns, like "I always fail" or "I shouldn't even try." Once you notice these thoughts, you can question them. Are they true? Are they fair? Or are they just old habits?

You stop ignoring your needs.

When you're aware of how you feel tired, stressed, and overwhelmed, you're more likely to treat yourself with care. That might mean saying no, taking a break, or asking for help. Every time you listen to your needs, you tell yourself, "I matter."

You set better boundaries.

Once you're aware of what drains you or hurts you, you can start setting limits. You don't have to explain or apologize for protecting your energy. That's self-respect in action, and it makes you feel secure and respected.

Try this simple awareness check-in today:

- When you feel upset, pause.
- Ask: What am I feeling?
- Ask again: What do I need?

At first, you might not know. That's okay. The more you practice, the easier it gets. Awareness is like a muscle; the more you use it, the stronger it becomes.

And don't worry if you slip into old habits. You will. That doesn't mean you're failing. It just means you're human. Awareness isn't about being perfect; it's about being honest.

Let's say you caught yourself saying something mean to yourself today, like, "Ugh, I'm so bad at this." Instead of pretending it didn't happen, pause. Notice it. Then try to speak back gently, like this: "I'm learning. It's okay to mess up. I'm doing my best."

That slight shift matters more than you think.

Self-respect also grows when you stop trying to meet everyone else's expectations and start listening to your own voice.

You might notice that you say "yes" when you want to say "no." Or that you push yourself to keep going when you're completely drained. Or that you pretend things are fine when they're not.

These patterns can feel normal, but they aren't helping you. When you ignore your own voice to please others, you lose trust in yourself. And confidence can't grow in a place where your own needs are always last.

Awareness helps you catch those moments and choose differently.

You might say, "Actually, I can't do that right now."

Or, "I need a break."

Or, "That doesn't feel right to me."

These are small sentences, but they build big strength. Each one is a message to yourself: I matter. My voice counts. I trust myself to make choices that are true for me.

Another part of awareness is noticing what *builds* you up.

What makes you feel strong?

What makes you feel calm or inspired?

Who do you feel like yourself around?

Pay attention to those things. They matter. When you start filling your life with people, activities, and thoughts that support you, your confidence grows naturally. You stop needing to "fix" yourself and start focusing on what fuels you.

Here's a simple practice to try today:

Awareness Practice: "Name it, and then choose."

1. Catch a thought or habit that feels unkind or unhelpful.

Example: "I'm such a mess today."

2. Name it without judgment.

"That's an old thought trying to keep me small."

3. Choose a new response.

"I'm having a hard day, and that's okay. I can take one step forward."

This practice doesn't erase old habits overnight, but it helps you see that you have a choice. And that choice builds confidence and respect from the inside out.

Repeat this thought to yourself today:

"I'm paying attention to how I treat myself. I deserve kindness from me."

Let this be your reminder that self-respect doesn't come from being tough or perfect. It comes from being aware. From noticing how you talk to yourself. From making choices that support your real needs.

You don't need to prove your worth.

You don't need to earn your place.

You just need to start seeing yourself clearly and treating yourself with the same care you'd give a friend.

That's how confidence grows.

One moment of self-awareness at a time.

One kind thought at a time.

One choice to respect yourself even just a little more every day.

Keep noticing. Keep choosing. Keep going.

You're doing better than you think.

WEEK 2: SHIFT HOW YOU SPEAK

Theme*: **Changing the Way You Talk to Yourself and Others***

The way you speak to yourself and to others shape how you see yourself. It affects your confidence more than you might realize. If your inner voice is constantly criticizing, doubting, or putting you down, it becomes harder to feel strong. But when your words are kind, honest, and supportive, they help you grow.

This week is about paying attention to the words you use and making small changes that build confidence, rather than tearing it down. For instance, instead of saying, "I'm so stupid," you could say, "I made a mistake, but I'm learning from it." this doesn't mean pretending everything is fine or being overly optimistic. It just means speaking to yourself with the same respect you'd give someone you care about.

Let's start with how you talk to *yourself*. Many people say things to themselves they'd never say to a friend. Things like, "I'm so stupid," "I always mess things up," or "Why can't I get it right?"

These thoughts might feel normal because they've been around for a long time. But just because they're common doesn't mean they're true or helpful.

The words you use become your beliefs. And your beliefs shape your actions. So if you're constantly telling yourself you're not good enough, you'll start to act like it. You might not try new things. You might stay quiet when you want to speak up. You might give up before you begin.

That's why this week is focused on shifting how you speak. When you start using words that support your growth, everything begins to feel different. Instead of saying, "I can't do this," try saying, "I'm still learning." Instead of "I always fail," try "I've had setbacks, but I'm still trying." These small shifts matter. They don't ignore your challenges; they help you keep going through them.

This week also includes how you speak *out loud* to friends, coworkers, family, and strangers. Do you downplay your ideas? Do you say "sorry" all the time, even when you didn't do anything wrong? Do you avoid sharing what you really think?

When you change the way you speak to others, you show more self-respect. You stop shrinking. You stop apologizing for existing. And even when it feels uncomfortable, you begin to show up more fully, which means expressing your thoughts and feelings without fear or hesitation.

Your voice matters. It doesn't have to be loud to be strong. What matters most is that it's true to you.

Each day this week, you'll focus on one small way to shift your words. You'll reflect on what you usually say, how that feels, and how to say something more helpful instead.

By the end of this week, you'll start to see the transformative potential of your words. They will begin to work *with* you, not against you, filling you with hope and optimism.

Remember, confidence begins with how you speak to yourself. Your inner dialogue is the foundation of your confidence, so make it strong and supportive.

And it grows every time you speak like you matter.

Because you do.

DAY 8: LISTENING TO YOUR INNER VOICE

Your inner voice is the way you talk to yourself when no one else is around. It's the quiet commentary running in the background of your mind, the part of you that notices how things are going and adds a comment or a judgment. Sometimes it cheers you on. Other times, it's full of doubt, fear, or criticism.

Today is about learning to *listen* to that voice.

Not so you can believe every word it says, but so you can start to understand where it's coming from, and whether it's helping you or holding you back.

Most people don't even realize how much their inner voice affects them. It's easy to move through the day without noticing how often you think things like, "I'm not good at this," or "I always mess up," or "They probably don't like me." But those thoughts add up. Even when you're not fully aware of them, they still influence how you feel and act.

Let's be clear: your inner voice is not *you*. It's just a part of your mind that's been shaped by the world around you. The voice in your head didn't show up out of nowhere. It was built over time from things you were told, things you saw, and moments that stuck with you.

Maybe someone once told you, "You're not that smart." Perhaps you failed a test and thought, "I guess I'm bad at this." Maybe you were ignored in a group and thought, "I must not matter."

Those thoughts might have started as reactions. But if you heard or felt them enough, your brain started repeating them. Not to hurt you, but to try to keep you safe. If your brain thought that being quiet or playing small would keep you from being embarrassed or rejected, it continued to do so.

But here's the problem: that old voice doesn't know the difference between real danger and new opportunity. It might still tell you to stay silent, even when you have something important to say. It might tell you to give up, even when you're doing just fine. It's trying to protect you, but it doesn't always know how to do that helpfully.

That's why listening is the first step. You can't change what you don't hear.

So today, just notice what your inner voice is saying.

You don't have to judge it or argue with it. Just notice. You might catch yourself thinking something like:

- "I'm too slow."
- "This is going to be a disaster."
- "I should've done better."
- "Why can't I get anything right?"

When that happens, pause and ask:

"Is this kind?"

"Is this helpful?"

"Would I say this to someone I care about?"

If the answer is no, then you know: this voice is not your truth, it's just an old pattern. You don't have to believe it.

You also don't have to replace it with fake positivity. You don't need to say, "Everything is amazing!" if that doesn't feel real. What matters more is shifting toward something *honest* and *gentle*.

Try saying, "I'm doing my best right now."

Or, "I can learn from this."

Or, "I've gotten through hard things before."

These statements are still true. But they're not harsh. They make space for growth instead of shutting you down.

You don't need to get rid of your inner voice. You just need to *train* it. You can teach your mind to speak to you in a new way, just like you'd train a muscle or learn a new skill.

Initially, the old voice may be louder. That's normal. It's been around longer. But the more you practice listening and choosing better words, the easier it gets to spot the difference between fear and truth.

Here's something to try today: carry a small notebook or open a notes app on your phone. Every time you notice your inner voice saying something critical, write it down. Then write a better version of that thought next to it.

For example:

- "I'm so bad at this." → "I'm still learning. That's okay."

- "I'm a mess." → "I've had a hard day, and I'm still showing up."
- "I can't do this." → "I can take one small step."

This exercise isn't about ignoring your struggles. It's about talking to yourself like someone who matters. Because you do.

And when your inner voice starts to reflect that? Everything changes.

You stop backing away from challenges.

You stop doubting yourself before you've even started.

You stop shrinking to make others comfortable.

You begin to trust yourself, just a little more each day.

Another helpful shift is to *name* your inner voice when it's being unkind. You don't have to call it "me." You can say, "Oh, there's that worried voice again," or, "That sounds like old fear talking."

Giving it a name helps create distance. It reminds you that this voice is not your whole identity; it's just a part of your thinking that you can work with and change over time.

And yes, it *does* change over time. Your brain is always learning. When you practice new thoughts and new patterns, it starts to catch on. Slowly, your inner voice becomes something more like a coach than a critic. It won't be perfect, but it'll be stronger, kinder, and more honest.

Today, give yourself permission to listen on purpose. Not to believe everything you hear but to notice it, challenge it, and begin to choose better words.

That's the work of real confidence. Not pretending you never have doubts, but learning to talk yourself through them instead of letting them dictate your decisions.

Keep listening.

Keep learning.

And remember: the voice in your head doesn't have to be the loudest one. You get to speak back.

DAY 9: REPLACE CRITICISM WITH HONESTY

EVERYONE HAS AN INNER VOICE. And on some days, that voice can sound like a bully. It points out every mistake, repeats old fears, and compares you to others. Instead of helping you grow, it holds you back. This voice often doesn't sound like the truth; it sounds like criticism.

But there's a better way to talk to yourself. You don't need to pretend everything is perfect. You don't need fake praise or forced positivity. What you need is *honesty*. Real, calm, kind honesty.

There's a big difference between criticism and honesty. Criticism attacks. Honesty observes. Criticism says, "You're terrible at this." Honesty says, "This part was hard for you today, and that's okay." Criticism makes you feel small. Honesty makes space for growth.

Let's take a closer look at how these two voices show up in everyday situations.

Say you forget something important, like a meeting or a task. The critical voice might say, "You're so irresponsible. You always screw things up." But honesty might say, "You forgot today. That doesn't mean you're irresponsible. You've had a lot on your mind. What can help you remember next time?"

See the difference?

The first voice tears you down. The second voice notices what happened and looks for a way to move forward. It still sees the truth but without the shame.

Or maybe you try something new and it doesn't go the way you hoped. The critical voice says, "You looked so dumb. You shouldn't have even tried." But honesty says, "That didn't go as planned. It was tough, but I'm proud I gave it a shot. Now I know what to try differently next time."

Honesty lets you keep your head up, even when things don't go perfectly.

So why do we use criticism at all?

For many people, harsh self-talk is a habit. Maybe you grew up hearing it from others. Maybe someone made you feel like you had to be perfect to be loved or noticed. Perhaps you thought that if you were hard on yourself, you'd avoid making mistakes.

But here's the truth: harshness doesn't build confidence. It builds fear. And when you're afraid of your own thoughts, it becomes harder to take risks, speak up, or grow.

You don't need to be hard on yourself to improve. You just need to be honest, aware, and gentle. That combination is what builds trust in yourself.

Let's break it down even more.

Criticism is full of extremes:

"You always mess this up."

"You'll never get it right."

"You're so bad at this."

Honesty uses facts, not exaggeration:

"You missed a detail here."

"This didn't turn out the way you wanted."

"You struggled today, and that's okay."

Criticism makes you feel hopeless. Honesty gives you direction.

The next time you hear yourself thinking something mean or harsh, pause and ask:

"Would I say this to someone I care about?"

If the answer is no, you can choose a better way to speak to yourself.

Let's say you're working on a goal, and it's taking longer than expected. The critical voice says, "You're lazy. You're never going to finish." But a more honest voice says, "You've slowed down lately. Maybe you're tired or overwhelmed. What's one thing you can do today to take a step forward?"

That's real support. And the best part? You can give it to yourself.

Another important shift is learning to replace *judgment* with *curiosity*.

Judgment says, "I failed again. I'm so bad at this."

Curiosity says, "What made this harder than I expected? What can I try differently next time?"

Judgment shuts you down. Curiosity opens up new options.

When you speak to yourself with honesty and curiosity, you create a more supportive space in your mind. That space makes it easier to take chances, learn from mistakes, and keep going even when things get tough.

Here's a quick example of how you can shift a critical thought into an honest one:

Critical thought: "I'm so behind. I should've done more by now."

Honest thought: "I've had a lot going on, and I'm still trying. I can make a small step today."

Critical thought: "Everyone else is better than me."

Honest thought: "I'm learning in my own way and at my own pace."

Critical thought: "I'm not good at anything."

Honest thought: "I'm still figuring out what I enjoy and where I want to grow."

These new thoughts don't lie to you. They just speak in a way that's more helpful and truer.

One way to get better at this is to write things down.

Try this:

1. At the end of your day, write down one critical thought you noticed.
2. Then write a new version of that thought, one that's honest but kind.
3. Say the new version out loud or quietly to yourself. Let it sink in.

The more you practice this, the easier it becomes to catch those harsh thoughts before they take hold. Over time, your brain starts to change. The honest voice becomes stronger. The critical one gets quieter.

And when that happens, confidence can grow.

Confidence doesn't mean you never struggle. It means you trust yourself enough to get through it without tearing yourself down.

When you speak to yourself kindly, you don't just feel better, you act differently. You take more chances. You're not as afraid to fail. You bounce back faster when things go wrong.

Because deep down, you know you're still on your side.

This is what today is all about: shifting from harshness to honesty. You don't need to be perfect to be proud of yourself. You just need to be honest enough to see where you are and kind enough to keep going.

So next time your inner voice starts to criticize, ask:

- "Is this helpful?"
- "Is this fair?"
- "What would I say to a friend in this situation?"

Then say that to yourself. Not because you're trying to sugarcoat the truth, but because the truth can be kind *and* clear.

And that's the kind of voice worth listening to.

Keep practicing. You're doing better than you think.

DAY 10: CHOOSING NEUTRAL OVER NEGATIVE

When something goes wrong, it's easy to be hard on yourself. Maybe you make a mistake. Perhaps something feels awkward or doesn't go as planned. Right away, your brain might go to a negative thought: "That was terrible," or "I'm so bad at this," or "Why did I even try?"

That's a habit. A very common one. Many people have trained their brains to go straight to negative thinking when things feel off. But here's the truth: You don't always have to choose between "good" and "bad." There's another option, and it's called *neutral*.

Neutral thinking means telling the truth about what happened without adding harsh judgment. It means seeing something clearly, without calling it good or bad. Instead of labeling your day as a failure, you can simply say, "That was a hard day." Instead of saying, "I messed everything up," you can say, "That didn't go how I wanted."

This small shift can make a huge difference in how you feel and how you act.

Let's say you give a short talk at school or work. Afterward, your brain starts replaying every tiny mistake. "I said the wrong word. I looked nervous. Everyone probably thought I sounded dumb." That's the negative voice showing up.

But if you practice neutral thinking, you pause and say something like, "I felt nervous. I forgot one part. But I got through it." That's the truth without shame, without drama, without attacking yourself.

Neutral thinking isn't pretending. It's not about ignoring your feelings or lying to yourself. It's just about *not making things worse* with harsh, negative thoughts.

Negative thinking adds pressure. It creates fear. It makes small moments feel like big failures. When that happens repeatedly, your confidence begins to wane. You stop trying. You avoid speaking up. You feel stuck.

But neutral thinking leaves space for growth.

Let's look at another example. Imagine trying something new, such as joining a club, speaking up in a meeting, or creating a video to share online. If you judge it right away and say, "That was embarrassing," or "I'm terrible at this," you might not try again.

But what if you said something neutral, like: "That was new for me," or "I'm learning," or "That was different from what I expected"? Those thoughts leave the door open. They remind you that one moment doesn't define you.

Neutral thinking gives you a break. It gives your brain space to breathe. It helps you step back, notice what happened, and move forward without all the extra weight of negativity.

Let's be clear, this doesn't mean you stop caring. It doesn't mean you stop trying to do your best. But it *does* mean you stop beating yourself up for being human.

Everyone has days that don't go well. Everyone makes mistakes. The difference is how you talk to yourself about it.

Try this:

1. The next time something goes wrong, notice your first thought.
2. Ask yourself: "Is this thought helping me, or just making me feel worse?"
3. Then try saying something neutral instead.

Here are a few examples of how to shift your thinking:

- **Negative:** "I messed everything up."
- **Neutral:** "I made a mistake. That's part of learning."
- **Negative:** "They probably think I'm stupid."
- **Neutral:** "I don't know what they think. I can only control what I do next."
- **Negative:** "I'm so bad at this."
- **Neutral:** "This is hard for me right now, but I'm working on it."
- **Negative:** "That was a disaster."
- **Neutral:** "That didn't go how I hoped, but I can try again."

See the pattern? Neutral thoughts don't sugarcoat the truth. They just leave out the harsh labels and allow you to keep going.

Why does this matter for confidence?

Because confidence is built through action, and action is easier when you're not afraid of your own thoughts.

If every mistake turns into a shame spiral, you'll avoid risks. You'll stay small. But if you can talk to yourself with calm, clear thoughts, even after things go wrong, you'll keep trying. And *that* is where confidence grows.

Consider athletes, artists, writers, or anyone who practices a particular skill. They don't improve by being perfect all the time. They improve by noticing what didn't work, adjusting, and trying again. They keep going, even when things don't feel great.

And how do they do that? By using more neutral, balanced thoughts.

You can do that too.

Here's another way to practice. At the end of your day, instead of thinking "Was today good or bad?" ask:

- What happened today that felt hard?
- What happened that surprised me?
- What am I learning about myself?

These questions move you away from judging and closer to understanding.

You can also write down a neutral thought and keep it where you'll see it often. Try one of these:

- "I can learn from this."
- "This moment doesn't define me."
- "One step at a time."
- "It's okay to feel uncomfortable and still keep going."

When your brain wants to jump to the worst conclusion, you'll have another option ready.

Over time, this gets easier. At first, it might feel strange. You might be so used to negative thoughts that they show up without you noticing. That's okay. The goal isn't to stop all your thoughts. The goal is to notice them and choose something better.

Remember, you're not trying to be fake-positive. You're choosing honest, clear thoughts that make space for growth. That's what neutral thinking is all about.

Here's a little practice you can try today:

- Think of something recent that made you feel bad.
- Write down the negative thought you had about it.
- Now, write a neutral version of that thought.
- Read it out loud. Let yourself hear a softer voice for once.

You don't need to be your own worst critic. You can be your own calm observer instead.

When you choose neutral over negative, you give yourself the chance to keep going. You build trust with yourself. You create a stronger, kinder mindset, one that lets you learn, grow, and try again without fear.

That's the heart of confidence. Not perfection. Not fake smiles. Just the steady belief that you can face hard things without tearing yourself down.

So today, pay attention to your thoughts. If one feels heavy or sharp, pause. Ask yourself, "Is there a more neutral way to say this?"

And then say it. To yourself. With honesty. With care.

You're not here to be perfect. You're here to keep showing up.

And choosing neutral? That's one of the strongest ways to do it.

DAY 11: SPEAKING TO YOURSELF WITH TRUST

When someone trusts you, how do they speak to you?

They're probably kind. Honest. They don't talk down to you, and they don't expect you to be perfect. They give you space to try, to mess up, to figure things out.

Now think about how *you* speak to yourself.

Is it patient? Supportive? Encouraging?

Or do you catch yourself saying things like:

- "Why can't I get this right?"
- "I'm probably going to mess this up."
- "No one is going to take me seriously."
- "I'm so behind."

Most people are way harder on themselves than they are on others. But if you're building confidence, that has to change. Today is about learning to speak to yourself with trust.

Confidence doesn't grow in a harsh, doubting voice. It grows in a voice that says, "I believe in you, even when it's hard."

You're not asking yourself to be perfect. You're asking yourself to *show up*. And that becomes much easier when the voice in your head feels like a friend, not an enemy.

So what does it mean to speak to yourself with trust?

It means you stop treating every mistake like proof that you're failing. It means you stop doubting yourself before you even try. And it means you start using words that help you move forward instead of staying stuck.

Let's look at a few examples of what that might sound like:

Instead of: "I probably won't get this right."

Try: "I'm learning something new. That's enough for now."

Instead of: "Everyone else is better at this than I am."

Try: "I'm on my own path. I don't have to be anyone else."

Instead of: "I'm so bad at this."

Try: "This is hard, but I've done hard things before."

When you talk to yourself with trust, you tell your brain, "I've got this. Maybe not perfectly, but I can handle it." And when your brain hears that enough times, it starts to believe it.

It's not about lying to yourself. It's about *telling the truth with kindness*.

For example, if you make a mistake, you don't need to pretend it didn't happen. You just speak to yourself in a way that still leaves room for hope.

- "That didn't go how I wanted, but I'm proud I tried."
- "I messed up, and now I know what to do differently next time."
- "That was tough, and I'm still here. I'm still showing up."

This kind of self-talk builds trust. It helps you keep trying, even when things feel hard, awkward, or slow. Because you're not tearing yourself down anymore. You're building yourself up, one word at a time.

Let's talk about the voice in your head.

It's always there. It's the one narrating your day. The one that notices when you stumble or feel unsure. And that voice can either make you feel safe... or make you feel small.

So many people live with an inner voice that says things like:

- "You're not ready."
- "You should've done better."
- "Why even bother?"

But you don't have to listen to that voice forever. You can train it to say different things. You can teach it to be calm, steady, and respectful. That's what speaking to yourself with trust really is.

Let's try something right now.

Think of something you've been nervous or unsure about. Maybe a decision you need to make, a conversation you want to have, or a goal you're working on. Notice what the voice in your head says about it. Is it doubting? Is it unkind?

Now, take a breath. Imagine the most patient person you know, someone who believes in you, no matter what. How would *they* talk to you in this moment?

That's the voice you can practice using for yourself.

You don't need to wait for someone else to say "You're doing great" or "I believe in you." You can say it to yourself. It might feel strange at first. That's okay. New habits always do. But the more you practice, the more normal it becomes.

Here are some trusted phrases you can start using:

- *"I trust myself to figure this out."*
- *"I can handle this one step at a time."*
- *"My effort matters more than being perfect."*
- *"I don't need to rush. I'm learning."*
- *"I'm allowed to try, even if I don't have all the answers."*

You can even write these down and put them somewhere you'll see them often, like your phone background, a sticky note on your mirror, or the first page of a journal.

Every time you see the words, say them out loud if you can. Let your body hear the sound of a voice that trusts you. Let your brain learn how that feels.

Because that's what confidence sounds like. Not shouting. Not showing off. But quiet belief in yourself.

Let's be real: There will still be days when doubt shows up. There will still be moments when you feel unsure or nervous or small. That's okay. You're human.

The goal isn't to eliminate doubt completely. The goal is to keep showing up, even when doubt is present, because the voice that trusts you is stronger now.

You might still think, "What if I mess up?" But now you can answer, "Then I'll learn from it, and I'll try again."

You might think, "I don't know what I'm doing." But you can follow it with, "And that's okay. I'm figuring it out."

That's what trust looks like in real life. Not having all the answers, but not giving up on yourself, either.

Today, take a moment to speak to yourself with trust. You don't need a big moment. You don't need a perfect plan. Just pick one small thing you've been hard on yourself about and try saying something kinder, truer, and more helpful.

Here's a practice to help you start:

1. Think of something that's been bothering you or making you doubt yourself.
2. Write down the negative thought that keeps popping up.
3. Ask yourself: "If someone I loved said this about themselves, how would I respond?"
4. Write *that* response down. That's your new self-talk.
5. Read it out loud. Let yourself hear it.

You can come back to this any time. This isn't a one-time thing; it's a habit you build. And with every kind word, every moment of patience, you're teaching yourself something important:

"I am someone I can trust."

That's the kind of confidence that lasts.

Keep going. Keep showing up. And keep speaking to yourself like someone who matters because you do.

DAY 12: REFRAMING "I CAN'T" AND "I'M NOT

WE ALL SAY things to ourselves that hold us back. Two of the most common phrases are: "I can't" and "I'm not." You've probably said them before without even thinking about it. Maybe you've told yourself, "I can't speak in front of people," or "I'm not confident," or "I'm not good at that." At first, these words might sound like facts. But they're usually not facts at all; they're habits.

The way we speak to ourselves becomes the way we see ourselves. If you repeat "I can't" or "I'm not" often enough, your brain starts to believe it's true. Even if you've never really tested it. Even if it's just something you picked up from someone else. Even if it only came from one bad experience.

But here's the good news: you don't have to keep repeating those old stories. You can learn to reframe those thoughts. That means turning them around in a way that gives you more room to grow. It's not about pretending everything is easy. It's about speaking to yourself in a way that lets you try.

Let's look at some examples.

If you catch yourself saying, "I can't do this," pause and ask: *Is that really true? Or is this just hard right now?* Then try shifting your words a little. You could say:

- "I don't know how to do this *yet*, but I'm learning."
- "This is new for me, and I'm figuring it out."
- "I'm not sure how to do this, but I can take a small step."

See the difference? Instead of shutting the door, you're opening it. You're not pretending everything is easy; you're just choosing a voice that keeps you going instead of stopping you.

"I'm not" is another phrase that can keep us stuck. For example, "I'm not confident," "I'm not creative," or "I'm not the kind of person who does that."

But the truth is, most "I'm not" statements are not fixed truths. They're beliefs are based on your past or on things people told you. And beliefs can change.

Consider this: just because you haven't done something yet doesn't mean you're incapable of it. Maybe you've just never had the chance. Maybe you were told you weren't good at something, so you stopped trying. That doesn't make it true.

Let's say you think, "I'm not confident." Ask yourself: *What does confidence even look like? Does it mean being loud all the time? Or does it mean showing up even when you feel unsure?*

You might already be more confident than you think.

Confidence can look quiet. It can look like trying something new. It can look like asking for help. It can look like making a mistake and trying again. So maybe it's not "I'm not confident." Maybe it's "I'm learning to trust myself more."

Here are some common "I can't" and "I'm not" thoughts and how to reframe them:

Instead of: "I can't speak in front of people."

Try: "Speaking in front of people makes me nervous, but I can practice."

Instead of: "I'm not good at talking to new people."

Try: "Talking to new people feels awkward for me, but I can get better at it with time."

Instead of: "I can't do this job."

Try: "This job challenges me, but I'm learning and improving."

Instead of: "I'm not creative."

Try: "I haven't explored my creativity yet, but I'm open to trying."

These new ways of thinking won't feel natural at first. That's okay. They're like new shoes; they might feel strange at the beginning, but the more you wear them, the more comfortable they get.

So why does this matter for confidence?

Because the words you use shape your beliefs. And your beliefs shape your actions. If you believe "I can't," you won't try. If you believe "I'm not," you won't step forward. But if you speak to yourself with curiosity and kindness, you give yourself a chance.

Let's say you're afraid to try something, like applying for a new role or starting a new hobby. If you say "I'm not ready," your brain backs off. It shuts the door. But if you say, "I don't feel ready, but I can learn as I go," you leave the door open just enough to try.

That's the difference between staying stuck and making progress.

Reframing isn't about lying to yourself. It's about speaking in a way that helps you keep moving.

Let's try a simple practice.

Step 1: Think of one thing you've been telling yourself you "can't" do.

Step 2: Write it down.

Step 3: Now ask yourself what's *really* true about this?

Step 4: Rewrite it in a way that's honest *and* hopeful.

Here's an example.

Original Thought: *"I can't do video calls. I always mess up what I want to say."*

Reframed Thought: *"Video calls make me nervous, but I can prepare ahead of time. I get a little better each time I try."*

This small change matters. It gives your brain something to work with. It creates space for growth. And it makes it easier to show up again tomorrow.

Here's something else to remember: most people you admire didn't start out as experts. They had to learn. They had to struggle. They had to do things they didn't think they could do until they could.

Confidence comes from doing things you once thought you couldn't. It grows when you take action, even when you're unsure.

So today, notice your "I can't" and "I'm not" thoughts. Don't judge yourself for having them. Everyone has them. But don't let them be the final word.

You always get to rewrite the story.

When you catch yourself thinking, "I can't," ask: *Is that really true? Or is it just unfamiliar?*

When you think, "I'm not," ask: *Is this something I've decided forever, or am I allowed to grow here?*

You are allowed to grow. You are allowed to try. You are allowed to say, "I'm learning," instead of "I'm failing."

And that small shift? It can change everything.

Daily Reminder:

The words you speak to yourself matter. They shape the way you think, the way you feel, and the way you move through the world. You don't have to be perfect. You just have to give yourself a chance.

So when you hear "I can't" or "I'm not," pause. Take a breath. Then say something truer. Something kinder. Something that gives you space to try.

That's how confidence begins. One word at a time.

DAY 13: STOP CALLING YOURSELF "TOO MUCH" OR "NOT ENOUGH

At some point, many of us have thought things like, "I'm too loud," or "I'm not smart enough," or "I care too much." These thoughts can come from small comments that stuck with us or from moments when we felt like we didn't fit in. Over time, they can become ingrained as beliefs about who we are and what we're allowed to be.

The truth is, most of these labels didn't start with us. They were picked up along the way from people who didn't understand us, or from a world that wanted us to be smaller, quieter, or easier to handle. But just because someone said you were "too much" or "not enough" doesn't mean it's true. Those words are not facts. They're opinions. And you don't have to carry them forever.

Let's look at what happens when we start believing these ideas.

If you've ever been told you're "too sensitive," you might have learned to hide your emotions. If someone said you're "too quiet," you may have started thinking your voice doesn't matter. If you were told you're "not athletic," "not pretty," "not smart," or "not brave," you may have stopped trying in those areas because you thought those parts of life just weren't for you.

But those are just labels. They're not the whole story. And they don't get to decide what you can or cannot do.

Here's the thing: people often say "too much" when they feel uncomfortable. If you cry easily, they say you're "too emotional." If you speak your mind, they say you're "too loud." If you set boundaries, they say you're "too difficult." But really, what they mean is, "I don't know how to handle this." That's about them, not you.

You don't have to shrink because someone else didn't know how to meet you with care.

And "not enough"? That's often a reflection of comparison. Maybe you looked around and felt like everyone else had it more together. Maybe someone made you feel small without even trying. Or perhaps you had a voice inside that told you you'd never measure up. However, what's most important is that you are not a problem to be fixed. You are a person growing.

Nobody is born "not enough." That belief gets learned. And because it's learned, it can also be unlearned.

It starts with noticing how often you say these things to yourself. When you think, "I'm not smart enough to do that," or "I care too much," pause and reflect. Ask yourself: *Where did that come from? Did someone say it once? Did I compare myself to someone else? Or am I just afraid I'll be judged?*

You may be surprised how often those thoughts are based on fear, not truth.

Now let's try something different. Let's turn "too much" and "not enough" into real qualities worth keeping.

- "Too sensitive" means you are aware of your feelings. You care. That's not weakness, it's kindness.
- "Too loud" might mean you have passion. You want to be heard. That matters.
- "Too quiet" could mean you think deeply. You don't rush to speak, but when you do, your words are thoughtful.
- "Not confident enough" might really mean, "I'm still learning to trust myself." That's a process, not a flaw.
- "Not outgoing enough" may mean, "I value one-on-one connections more than big crowds." That's just a different style, not something to fix.

You don't need to fit one version of who you're "supposed" to be. You just need to be honest about who you are and trust that that's enough.

Let's try an exercise.

Think of one thing you've called yourself recently, something like "too much" or "not enough."

Now write it down. Look at it closely.

Ask yourself:

- Who taught me this?
- Was it said to me, or did I say it after comparing myself to someone else?
- What is this belief costing me?

Next, write a new version. One that gives you space to grow.

For example:

"I'm too emotional" becomes "I feel deeply, and that helps me connect with others."

"I'm not brave enough" becomes "I feel scared sometimes, but I've done brave things before, and I can do them again."

This isn't about pretending hard things are easy. It's about being fair to yourself. You don't need to tear yourself down to stay humble. You can accept where you are, while still being proud of what you're becoming.

Here's another thing to think about: when you say something mean to yourself, would you say it to someone else? Would you tell a friend, "You're not good enough," or "You care too much"? Probably not. So, why speak to yourself that way?

You deserve the same care you give to others. Maybe even more.

Confidence grows when you stop repeating the old stories that never helped you. It grows when you stop holding yourself to impossible rules like "Don't take up too much space," or "Don't ask for too much," or "Don't want more than you deserve."

You can be a work in progress and still be worthy right now. You can have doubts and still move forward. You can be quiet, or bold, or somewhere in between, and still matter.

Your voice matters. Your feelings matter. Your hopes, your goals, your way of showing up in the world, all of that matters.

And no one gets to decide that you're "too much" or "not enough."

Not a teacher. Not a parent. Not a boss. Not a friend. Not a stranger.

You decide how you speak to yourself. You decide how much space you take up.

You are allowed to be proud of who you are, without waiting for permission. You are allowed to grow, without calling yourself names along the way.

So today, take a breath. And try saying this:

"I am not too much. I am not enough. I am just right where I am. And I'm growing."

Say it again tomorrow. Say it the next day, too. Even if you don't believe it yet. Even if it feels strange. Words can shape the way you feel. Give them time.

You don't have to be perfect. You don't have to change your whole self. But you do have to stop being mean to yourself.

Because the real truth is: You were never too much. You were never not enough. You were just told the wrong story.

And now, you get to write a new one.

DAY 14: QUIET STRENGTH IN EVERYDAY SPEECH

When most people think of confidence, they imagine someone who speaks loudly, takes up a lot of space, or always knows exactly what to say. But real confidence doesn't always look that way. In fact, some of the strongest people speak with calm voices. Some of the clearest people don't talk a lot. And some of the most powerful words are spoken gently, without needing to shout.

Confidence isn't about being the loudest voice in the room. It's about understanding that you don't need to be loud to be heard. It's about believing in the significance of your voice, even if it's soft. It's about presenting your true self, without the need to impress anyone.

This is called quiet strength. And you might already have it.

Quiet strength isn't about hiding. It's not about staying small or staying silent. It's about speaking from a place of truth. It's about choosing your words with care. And it's about staying calm and grounded, even when things feel a little shaky inside.

You may have seen quiet strength before and not even realized it. It's the person who doesn't speak often, but when they do, people listen. It's the friend who helps others without making a big show of it. It's the classmate or coworker who doesn't argue just to win, but who speaks clearly when it matters most.

You can show quiet strength in many small ways throughout your day.

You show it when you say "no" without explaining yourself again and again. You show it when you disagree politely. You show it when you stand up for someone, even if it's awkward. You show it when you say something honest, even if it makes your voice shake. You even show it when you take a breath instead of rushing to fill the silence.

Embracing quiet strength may not always be easy. It can feel uncomfortable, especially if you're used to apologizing for everything or trying to say the "right" thing to avoid upsetting others. But as you start to speak with quiet strength, you'll notice a significant shift. You'll feel less like you're performing and more like you're just being yourself, which brings a sense of comfort and ease.

That's where real confidence lives.

Let's look at a few ways you can use quiet strength in how you speak.

First, pause before you speak. You don't have to rush. Taking a moment to think before you answer gives your words more weight. It also shows that you respect your thoughts enough to choose them carefully.

Second, drop the extra apologies. If you've done something wrong, of course, say sorry. But many people say "sorry" when they haven't done anything wrong. "Sorry for asking this…" or "Sorry if I'm bothering you…" These sound polite, but they also send a message that you think your voice is a problem. Try replacing "sorry" with "thank you." For example, "Thank you for your patience," instead of "Sorry I'm late."

Third, speak clearly, even if it's brief. You don't need to say a lot to say something meaningful. If you have an opinion, you're allowed to share it without trying to soften it for others. You don't need to add "just," "maybe," or "I could be wrong but…" to every sentence. Speaking clearly doesn't make you rude; it shows that you trust your thoughts.

Fourth, use your voice to support others. Quiet strength also means speaking up when someone else needs support. You don't have to give a long speech. Sometimes, simply saying, "I agree," or "That's not okay," can change the entire tone of a conversation. You don't need to be loud to be a leader.

Fifth, don't be afraid of silence. Many people talk quickly or fill the quiet because they're nervous. But silence isn't bad. It gives people space to think. It gives your words time to land. When you get comfortable with silence, you start feeling less rushed and more at ease.

And finally, speak to yourself with the same steady tone. The voice in your head matters just as much as the one others hear. Quiet strength starts from the inside. If you're always putting yourself down in your own mind, it's harder to speak with confidence out loud. Practice saying simple, kind things to yourself: "I handled that well." "I said what I meant." "I spoke clearly." These thoughts cultivate inner steadiness, which is reflected in how you interact with others.

You don't need to change who you are to speak with strength. You don't need to pretend to be louder, bolder, or more dramatic. You can be steady. You can be thoughtful. You can be yourself. Quiet confidence is just as real as loud confidence. Sometimes, it's even stronger because it comes from a deeper, more authentic place.

Let's look at a few examples of quiet strength in action.

A student sits in class and listens closely. When the teacher asks a question, they don't raise their hand right away. But when they do, they speak clearly and say something honest. That's quiet strength.

A friend in a group feels like the conversation is going in a direction that doesn't feel right. They don't yell. They don't argue. They just say, "I think we should talk about something else." That's quiet strength.

A person in a meeting has an idea. They're nervous, but they speak anyway. They don't shout. They don't try to win everyone over. They just say, "Here's something I've been thinking about." That's quiet strength.

You might already be doing these things without realizing it. This may be new to you. Either way, you can build this kind of strength, one word at a time.

Here's a simple way to practice:

Select one moment in your day when you typically remain silent, over-apologize, or speak too quickly. In that moment, pause. Breathe. Then speak slowly and clearly. Don't add extra words. Don't rush. Just say what you mean.

At the end of the day, reflect. How did it feel? What worked? What was uncomfortable? This kind of reflection helps your confidence grow, not because you were perfect, but because you stayed true to yourself.

Confidence isn't always about speaking louder. Sometimes, it's about speaking less, but meaning every word. Sometimes, it's about saying something simple and standing by it. Sometimes, it's about not saying anything at all but still knowing you belong.

That's quiet strength.

And it lives in you.

WEEK 3: SHIFT HOW YOU SHOW UP

Theme: ***Practicing confidence in real-world actions***

You've already begun to shift how you think and speak. This week, it's time to take those changes out into the real world. Confidence grows when you act on what you believe, not just in your mind, but through your choices, your body language, and your daily actions. You don't have to be perfect. You just have to be willing to show up.

This week is all about practicing confidence in small, doable ways. You'll learn how to walk into a room as if you belong, how to make a clear request, and how to hold your ground even in moments that feel uncomfortable. These aren't big, dramatic changes. They're small actions that build trust in yourself over time.

Confidence isn't always a feeling. Sometimes, it's a behavior. You might not feel brave, but you can still take a brave action. You might not feel confident, but you can still show up and do the thing. And when you do, something important happens: your brain learns, "Oh, I can handle this."

This is how real change happens. Not all at once, but moment by moment. Step by step.

This week, pay attention to how you carry yourself in everyday situations. Do you walk in with your head down, hoping no one notices you? Or do you allow yourself to take up space? Do you shrink your voice in meetings, or do you speak clearly even when you're nervous? These choices send messages to your own brain and to the people around you about what you believe you deserve.

You'll also be practicing boundaries this week. That includes learning to say "no" without guilt and saying "yes" without needing permission. You'll explore what it feels like to speak with a steady pace. To pause instead of rushing. To trust that you are allowed to be here.

Sometimes, the most significant shift isn't what you say or do, it's how you *stand* while you're doing it. It's the choice to breathe before you speak. It's making eye contact. It's giving a firm answer instead of a hesitant one. It's asking for something you need, even when you're scared someone might say no.

These actions may feel small on the outside, but they're powerful. Every time you take a step that honors your voice, your values, or your needs, you build confidence. And the more you do it, the more natural it becomes.

So this week, pay attention to how you move through your day. Show up a little more fully. Speak up a little more clearly. And remember: you don't need to feel 100% ready to act with confidence.

You just need to start.

Because showing up isn't about being fearless, it's about showing yourself that you don't have to hide anymore.

DAY 15: SAY WHAT YOU MEAN

Confidence doesn't always come from big speeches or bold moves. Often, it begins in small, everyday moments like choosing to say what you actually mean. That might sound simple, but it's one of the most powerful ways to build real trust in yourself. Most people have been in a situation where they said something they didn't really mean. Maybe they said "yes" to a favor they didn't want to do. Perhaps they laughed at a joke that didn't quite land. Or maybe they stayed quiet when they wanted to speak up. These aren't just little habits. They are ways we train ourselves to hide.

Saying what you mean doesn't mean saying everything that comes to mind. It doesn't mean being rude or unfiltered. It means telling the truth kindly and clearly. It means letting your words match your thoughts. When you say what you mean, people start to know and trust the real you, and you start to trust yourself more, too. The more you match your words to your truth, the less you'll feel like you're performing. You won't walk away from conversations feeling like you betrayed yourself. You'll feel stronger, clearer, and more grounded in your identity.

So why do we avoid saying what we mean? One big reason is fear. We're afraid of hurting someone's feelings, making a situation awkward, or being judged. We're taught to be polite and easy to get along with, and sometimes that gets confused with being agreeable at all costs. Another reason is habit. If you've been taught to keep the peace, you may not even realize you're hiding your real thoughts. You say yes without thinking. You downplay what you want. You soften every sentence so it doesn't sound "too direct." Over time, this makes your voice feel smaller. And when your voice feels small, your confidence does too.

There's also a fear of being seen. Saying what you mean is a kind of honesty that leaves you open. When you say "I disagree," "I need help," or "I don't like that," you're showing more of who you are. That can feel risky. But it's also freeing. Being honest in your speech means you stop needing to manage other people's opinions. You stop shaping your words to please or protect someone else. You focus on being real, not just being liked.

You don't have to be blunt or harsh to speak clearly. In fact, the strongest kind of honesty is steady, kind, and calm. You can say, "I'd rather not," without explaining yourself for five minutes. You can say, "I'm not comfortable with that," without sounding like you're starting a fight. You can say, "That's not right for me," and leave it there. Clear communication shows confidence because it tells the world that you trust your own voice. You don't need to convince anyone else. You're standing in your own truth.

Saying what you mean also helps with boundaries. When your words reflect your real limits, people are less likely to push them. Saying, "I can't take that on right now," is clearer than, "I'll try, but no promises." Saying, "That doesn't work for me," is more honest than saying, "Maybe," when you really mean no. Clear speech helps people know where you stand. And it helps you feel more in control of your time and energy.

One way to begin is by noticing where you usually soften or hide your words. Do you say "I don't know" when you actually do? Do you say "I'm fine" when you're not? Do you say "It's okay" when something hurts you? Start paying attention. These tiny moments matter. They're the places where your confidence grows or shrinks. Every time you speak clearly, even about something small, you remind yourself that your voice matters.

You don't have to fix this all at once. Start with one moment a day. If someone asks how you're doing, simply tell the truth. If you're asked for your opinion, share it honestly, even if it's different. If you don't want to do something, say no kindly. These may feel like small shifts, but they build something big. They build a version of you who feels strong enough to be real, even when it's a little uncomfortable.

If you're worried about how others will respond, remember this: you don't control how people take your words. You only control how you show up. If you speak with respect and care, that's all that's needed. Some people may be surprised when you stop always agreeing or always smoothing things over. That's okay. You're not here to keep others comfortable at your own expense. You're here to live as your authentic self.

Sometimes, it helps to rehearse. If you know a conversation is coming where you'll need to say something honest, practice it out loud first. Write it down if you need to. Saying your words ahead of time makes it easier to speak them in the moment. And if your voice shakes or your heart races, that's still okay. Speaking up is still brave, even when it feels hard.

Confidence doesn't mean never feeling nervous. It means doing what matters, even when you do. And speaking your truth is one of those things that matters. Not because every conversation needs to be perfect, but because every time you match your words with your truth, you stop hiding. You stop pretending. And you build something stronger in its place.

If you slip into old habits, don't beat yourself up. You've spent years learning to soften or shape your voice. It's normal for this to take practice. Just notice the moment. Ask yourself, "What did I really want to say?" And try again next time. Growth doesn't come from getting it right every time. It comes from being willing to keep trying.

Here's something to try today: pick one moment where you usually hide or soften your voice. It might be when someone asks for your help, or when a friend says something you disagree with, or when someone crosses a boundary. Decide ahead of time what you want to say in that moment. Keep it short, clear, and kind. Then say it. Even if your heart beats fast. Even if it feels strange. Say what you mean.

End the day by reflecting on how that felt. Did you feel clearer? Did you feel more honest? Did you feel proud of yourself? You don't need the other person to agree with you to feel good. What matters most is that you showed up for yourself. And that's what builds real confidence.

Saying what you mean is one of the most respectful things you can do for yourself and others. It takes practice. It takes courage. But it's worth it. Every time you speak honestly, you stand taller. You trust yourself more. And you invite others to meet the real you. That's confidence in action. And it begins with your words.

DAY 16: MAKE ONE BOLD ASK

THERE'S something powerful about asking for what you need. It might sound simple, but many people go years without doing it. Not because they don't have needs, ideas, or goals, but because asking feels scary. What if the answer is no? What if they think I'm too much? What if I seem needy, greedy, or ungrateful? These thoughts are common, and they're exactly why today's practice is so essential: making one bold ask.

A bold ask doesn't have to be big or dramatic. It just has to feel like a stretch for you. It's something you would normally talk yourself out of. Maybe it's asking your boss for more support. Maybe it's reaching out to someone you admire and asking for a meeting. Maybe it's asking a friend to show up for you in a new way. Maybe it's asking for help with something you've been trying to carry on your own. It doesn't matter what it is; it matters that you ask.

Why is this so tied to confidence? Because asking means you believe you're worth the time, help, opportunity, or attention. You're stepping into a mindset that says, "I am allowed to take up space. I'm allowed to want something. I'm allowed to ask for more." Even if the answer is no, the act of asking is already a win. You've already grown just by doing it.

One of the biggest reasons people don't ask is fear of rejection. It's a fear that goes deep, because when we're told no, it can feel like we're being told *we're* not enough. But the truth is, rejection is just an answer, not a reflection of your worth. Everyone hears no sometimes. Confident people hear it too. They just don't take it as proof that they shouldn't have asked in the first place. They know that not every door will open, but they also know they'll never find the open ones if they don't knock.

Another reason people avoid asking is that they don't want to seem like a burden. This often comes from growing up in environments where needing something was seen as a weakness or an inconvenience. If you learned to always figure things out on your own, you might think it's stronger to stay silent. But real strength includes knowing when to reach out. You're not supposed to do everything alone. You're allowed to ask for support, resources, connection, or opportunity. That doesn't make you weak. It makes you human.

You might also fear seeming "too much." Too ambitious. Too bold. Too forward. But that fear often keeps people stuck in lives that are smaller than what they truly want. Confidence grows when you let yourself be seen, when you risk being misunderstood, and when you step forward instead of holding back. A bold ask says, "I believe I matter even if it's uncomfortable to show it."

Today's practice isn't about getting a yes. It's about building your voice. It's about getting used to the feeling of asking, even when you don't know how it'll go. And the more you do it, the easier it becomes. Your fear shrinks. Your belief in yourself grows. And you start realizing you can handle whatever comes next, yes, no, or maybe.

If you're not sure what to ask for, here are a few examples to get you thinking:

- Ask someone for feedback on something you care about.
- Ask a colleague or mentor for help with a skill you'd like to develop.
- Ask a friend for emotional, practical, or other types of support.
- Ask your boss for clearer boundaries or more growth opportunities.
- Ask to be included in a project, opportunity, or decision.
- Ask someone to consider your needs in a situation where they usually don't.
- Ask for time, space, or help without apologizing for it.

Think about something you've wanted but haven't asked for. What stopped you? Was it fear of seeming needy? Worry about rejection? Uncertainty about how to phrase it? Those are all normal blocks, but they're not the final ones. You can move through them with practice. And today, that's exactly what you're doing.

If asking out loud feels too hard right away, write it down first. Practice it. Get clear on what you want to say. Be direct, but respectful. Be honest, but thoughtful. You don't need to explain your entire life story. You can just say:

- "I need help with something. Can we talk?"
- "I've been thinking about this for a while, and I'd like to ask for your support."
- "Would you be willing to consider...?"
- "I'm reaching out because I value your input, and I'd love to ask you something."

- "This might be a long shot, but I'd regret not asking."

Those sentences open the door. What matters most is that you speak from a place of self-respect, not desperation. Not begging. Not people-pleasing. Just clarity and honesty.

It's also important to remember: other people have their own limits, timing, and priorities. A no is not personal. A no doesn't mean you were wrong to ask. It just means the fit wasn't right this time, or with this person. Don't let one no shut you down. If you keep asking, your voice gets stronger. Your direction gets clearer. And eventually, the right people, places, and opportunities begin to show up.

You might be surprised by how often a bold ask gets a yes. People want to help more than you think. But they can't say yes if you don't give them the chance. Being brave enough to ask shows courage, trust, and maturity. It shows that you're not waiting around for life to hand you something; you're taking part in shaping it.

And here's something else: bold asks don't just build confidence. They build a connection. When you ask someone for help, or a chance, or support, you give them a role in your story. That creates closeness. That builds trust. Asking can feel vulnerable, but it's one of the fastest ways to build stronger relationships.

Today, your task is to make one bold ask. Don't wait until you feel ready. Don't wait until the perfect moment. Pick one thing, and ask. Say it. Send the message. Schedule the meeting. Make the call. Take the step.

And then notice how it feels. Maybe your heart races. Maybe your voice shakes. That's okay. Bold doesn't mean fearless. Bold means you did it anyway.

At the end of the day, write about the experience. What did you ask for? What emotions came up for you: fear, excitement, guilt, or pride? What happened? What did you learn?

Whether you get a yes, no, or something in between, you'll know one thing for sure: you showed up for yourself today. You said, "I'm worth asking." And that's what real confidence is made of.

Keep building that voice. Keep practicing those asks. Because the more you speak up for what you need, the more life begins to meet you there.

And remember: the boldest part isn't getting the yes. It's choosing to believe that your voice matters enough to ask at all.

DAY 17: HOLD YOUR GROUND IN SMALL MOMENTS

Confidence doesn't always arrive with a big speech or a bold decision. More often, it shows up quietly in the small, everyday moments where you choose to stay true to yourself. The moment you say no, even when it would have been easier to say yes. The moment you speak up gently instead of staying silent. The moment you keep your boundary without guilt. These little choices don't get applause, but they are where your real strength is built.

It's easy to picture confidence as something flashy: commanding a room, giving a powerful presentation, or taking a huge risk. But those moments don't happen often. What happens every day are the smaller ones the conversations, decisions, and interactions where you get to decide: Will I shrink, or will I stay steady? Will I surrender myself to maintain the peace, or will I trust myself enough to stand firm?

To hold your ground means to stand by your values, your needs, and your truth, even when it's uncomfortable. It doesn't mean being rigid or harsh. It doesn't mean turning every moment into a fight. It means knowing what matters to you, and being willing to stay connected to that even if someone else doesn't like it.

Holding your ground might mean turning down a project at work when your plate is already full. It might mean saying, "Actually, I don't agree," in a conversation where everyone else nods along. It might mean asking for space when you need time to think, or calmly reminding someone of a boundary you've already set. These aren't dramatic moments. They're everyday situations where you quietly choose self-respect over self-abandonment.

Why do we so often give in during these small moments? Because we've been taught that going along is easier. Many of us were raised to be polite, agreeable, and easy to work with. Somewhere along the way, we learned that making others comfortable was more important than staying true to ourselves. So we nod. We say yes. We say it's fine when it isn't. We let things slide.

But the cost of constantly giving in is that you slowly lose trust in yourself. You stop feeling like your voice matters. You begin to doubt whether your needs are valid. And each time you back down, a little part of you learns, "Maybe I can't be counted on to speak up for myself." That's not a lesson you want to keep learning.

The good news? You can change that message. You can start holding your ground, one small moment at a time. And with each moment, you rebuild your own trust. You start to believe: I can speak up. I can stay steady. I don't have to give myself away to stay connected to others.

So what does this actually look like?

Let's say you're in a meeting and someone interrupts you. Instead of shrinking or letting it slide, you pause and say, "I'd like to finish my thought." It's a simple sentence, but it signals something powerful you're not willing to disappear.

Or maybe a friend invites you out, but you're tired. Instead of saying yes out of guilt or obligation, you say, "Thanks for the invite, but I need a night to rest." You don't apologize. You don't over-explain. You just say what's true.

Or maybe someone asks you to do something you don't have time or energy for. Instead of automatically agreeing, you pause and say, "I'm not available to take that on right now." You're still kind, but you're also clear.

These are all ways of holding your ground respectful, calm, and steady.

Holding your ground doesn't mean being unkind or argumentative. In fact, the strongest form of confidence often comes with a sense of softness. You can be firm and still be warm. You can say no without being rude. You can disagree without being dramatic. Confidence isn't about volume it's about alignment.

That means your words match your truth. You don't say "yes" when you mean "no." You don't laugh off something that actually hurts. You don't pretend to be okay just to keep others comfortable. You honor what's real for you, even when it's awkward. Even when it's quiet. Even when no one else notices.

Because you notice. And that matters.

Confidence isn't something you earn by being perfect. It's something you grow by staying close to yourself especially in the moments when it would be easier not to. The more you do that, the stronger you get. You stop being so shaken by others' opinions. You stop needing everyone to agree. You stop second-guessing every little thing.

Instead, you become the kind of person who knows: I can trust myself to stay rooted. I can hold my ground, even when it's hard.

Here's something helpful to try. The next time you feel yourself hesitating about a request, a comment, a boundary pause and ask:

- What do I actually want to say?
- What would I say if I trusted myself more?
- What will I feel like later if I say yes when I mean no?

These quick questions bring you back to yourself. They give you a moment to choose not react out of habit. And that moment of awareness is powerful. It's where confidence lives.

Sometimes, people will push back when you hold your ground. They might not be used to you saying no. They might expect you to give in. That's okay. You don't have to convince anyone. You're not here to make everyone like your boundaries. You're here to trust them.

Your job is to keep practicing. Not perfectly. Just more often. Every time you hold your ground in a small moment, you build strength for the big ones. It's like lifting weights you get stronger with each rep. Even if it's awkward at first. Even if your voice shakes.

And if you do back down sometimes? That's okay too. Confidence doesn't mean getting it right every time. It just means staying aware. Learning from it. Trying again.

So today, your challenge is this: find one small moment to hold your ground. Say what you mean. Say no if you need to. Ask for what matters. Pause before responding. Stay connected to your truth, even if it's just in a small sentence.

And afterward, reflect. How did it feel? What did you learn? What happened? Let yourself feel proud not because it was perfect, but because it was real.

Confidence doesn't need a spotlight. It just needs practice. One moment at a time.

You're doing it. Keep going. Keep showing up. Keep holding your ground. Because your voice matters even when it's quiet. Especially when it's quiet.

DAY 18: SPEAKING WITH STEADY PACE AND CLARITY

HAVE you ever noticed how quickly your words start to tumble out when you're nervous? Maybe your heart is racing, and your thoughts are moving faster than your mouth can keep up. You might stumble over your words, talk too fast, or forget what you were trying to say altogether. These moments are more common than you think and they don't mean you're not confident. But learning to speak with a steady pace and clarity can help you *feel* more confident, and help others see you that way, too.

Speaking with clarity isn't just about sounding good. It's about giving yourself room to breathe, space to think, and the chance to express your ideas fully. It's about slowing down not to drag out your words, but to make sure they land the way you want them to. When you speak clearly and calmly, people tend to listen more attentively. They not only hear you they trust you more. And most importantly, you begin to trust yourself.

There's a natural urge to rush when we're unsure. We try to get our words out fast so we don't get interrupted or judged. But in doing so, we sometimes send the message that we don't fully believe in what we're saying. Fast, jumbled speech can come across as unsure or apologetic even when your message is strong. On the other hand, speaking slowly and clearly signals self-assurance. It shows that you believe your words matter enough to be said with care. This is not just about communication, it's about empowerment. It's about taking control of your narrative and making sure your voice is heard.

Let's be clear: slowing down doesn't mean dragging your sentences or talking in a forced, unnatural way. It means pacing yourself so that you can stay connected to your thoughts and ideas. It means giving yourself the space to complete one idea before moving on to the next. And it means allowing your listener to absorb your words without feeling rushed or confused.

Here's what often happens when you start speaking with more clarity: You feel more grounded. You make fewer mistakes. You give yourself time to think. And you begin to notice how much more effective your communication becomes. People lean in instead of zoning out. You stop second-guessing every sentence. You feel calm, instead of scrambling to say things before you lose your chance.

Of course, changing your speaking habits takes time. If you've spent years rushing through conversations or shrinking your voice to stay out of the spotlight, this will feel awkward at first. That's okay. Growth always feels awkward before it feels natural.

Start with self-awareness. Notice when you begin to speed up. Pay attention to the times your speech becomes rushed or choppy. Is it in meetings? On phone calls? Around certain people? The more you understand your patterns, the more you can begin to shift them. Remember, self-awareness is the first step towards improvement.

Here are a few simple ways to start speaking with a steadier pace and clarity:

Breathe Before You Speak

It sounds simple, but many people forget to take a full breath before they start talking. A breath helps calm your nerves and center your thoughts. It slows you down and helps you begin with intention, rather than panic. Try inhaling deeply before answering a question or making a point. You'll be surprised how different it feels.

Pause Between Sentences

You don't need to fill every second with sound. Pauses are powerful. They give your listener time to absorb what you've said. They also give *you* a chance to regroup and decide what to say next. Think of pauses as part of your message not a gap in it.

Use Shorter Sentences

When you're nervous, you might try to say everything in one long, breathless sentence. But long sentences can get confusing for both you and your listener. Try breaking your ideas into shorter, simpler thoughts. Say one thing clearly, and then move to the next.

Focus on Enunciation

Sometimes people mumble or trail off when they don't feel confident. Practice saying your words fully. Enunciate clearly, even if it feels unnatural at first. This helps your speech sound stronger and allows your message to come through more clearly.

Slow Down Your Pace Gently

You don't need to talk like you're reading a script. Just aim to slow down your natural rhythm by a small degree. Talk like you're having a thoughtful conversation with someone who matters and who really wants to understand you.

The goal isn't to be perfect. It's to practice. Speaking clearly is a skill you can build, not something you're either "good" or "bad" at. With time, it will feel more natural. You'll notice your thoughts come together more easily. You'll start to feel less anxious in conversations. You might even begin to enjoy speaking up; because you won't be rushing to the end you'll be present for the middle.

This also helps with boundaries. When you speak slowly and clearly, you're more likely to say what you actually mean, instead of blurting something out that you later regret. This can be particularly useful in professional settings, such as during presentations or negotiations. You give yourself a chance to respond instead of react. This can make hard conversations go more smoothly and help you hold your ground with more ease.

You'll also notice that people respond to you differently. They may interrupt you less. They may lean in more. They may repeat your words later because they actually *heard* what you said. You don't need to shout to get attention. You just need to speak with intention.

Confidence in speech isn't about how loud you are. It's about how connected you are to what you're saying. When you trust yourself, your voice follows. When you give your words weight, others begin to give them weight, too. This is the essence of self-assured communication. It's not just about the words you speak, but the trust you have in yourself to speak them. When you believe in your message, others will too.

Here's a practice you can try:

Choose a short paragraph or a few sentences from a book or article you like. Read it out loud slowly, paying attention to your pace, pauses, and tone of voice. Then, choose a few thoughts of your own and speak them out loud in the same way. For example, say: "I'm learning to speak with clarity. My voice matters. I don't need to rush." Notice the difference between speaking slowly and clearly versus speaking quickly and anxiously. Let yourself feel the difference in your body, too.

You might also try recording yourself speaking just for you. Listen back without judgment. What do you notice? Where do you rush? Where do you sound calm? This is not about being critical; it's about getting familiar with your own voice and learning how to support it.

Remember: clarity takes practice. You're allowed to stumble. You're allowed to pause. You're allowed to start over. The more you do this, the easier it gets. And as it gets easier, you'll notice something shift not just in your speech, but in how you feel about yourself.

So today, when you speak, try slowing down a little. Take a breath before you begin. Pause between thoughts. Let your words carry weight. You're not rushing to the end you're showing up for the moment.

Speak like someone worth listening to. Because you are.

DAY 19: WALKING INTO SPACES LIKE YOU BELONG

Have you ever walked into a room whether it's a meeting, a class, a party, or even a group chat and immediately felt like you didn't fit in? That awkward moment when you wonder if you're over-dressed or underdressed, if you've said the wrong thing, or if you should even be there at all? That feeling is more common than most people are willing to admit. And it doesn't come from a lack of ability it comes from a learned belief that your presence has to be earned.

But the truth is this: you belong in every room you walk into, not because of your resume or your confidence level or how polished you are, but because you are a whole, valuable person. Belonging isn't something someone else gives you. It's something you decide for yourself.

Most of the time, the people who seem "naturally confident" aren't necessarily more talented or prepared. They've just learned to show up with the belief that they belong, even when they feel nervous. That belief walking into a space like you belong is what we're focusing on today. Because when you carry that energy, the world tends to meet you differently.

Many of us carry memories from childhood, school, or early work experiences that taught us to be smaller, quieter, or more agreeable to fit in. You learned to scan the room for cues: how are people dressed? What are they saying? Should I speak up or stay quiet? Over time, this scanning becomes second nature. You start trying to mold yourself into something you think people will accept instead of showing up as who you are.

The problem is, constantly adapting for approval keeps you disconnected from yourself. You spend so much time performing, adjusting, or doubting that you don't give yourself the chance to truly connect. Confidence comes from alignment not perfection. And alignment means showing up as yourself, not someone else.

Walking into a space like you belong isn't about arrogance or dominance. It's not about taking over. It's about walking with a quiet, steady sense that you don't need to prove anything to deserve your spot. You deserve to be in the room because you're human, you're trying, and you're here to learn or contribute just like everyone else.

Your posture matters. Your breathing matters. Your energy matters. When you walk in with your head up, shoulders relaxed, and an open heart, people notice. They may not consciously register it, but your presence communicates something. It says, "I'm here, and I'm not shrinking." That doesn't mean you won't feel nervous. But you don't let that nervousness lead the way.

When you doubt your belonging, your body often responds first. You may find yourself physically shrinking crossing your arms, looking down, pulling your shoulders in, making yourself smaller. This isn't a weakness. It's a survival habit. Your nervous system is trying to keep you safe by minimizing your exposure to danger. But this habit can also hold you back from connecting, speaking, or taking up space in meaningful ways.

Try this slight shift: before you enter a space, pause and check in with your body. Roll your shoulders back. Take one deep breath. Say to yourself, "I belong here." Then walk in with that message running quietly in the background. You don't need to fake confidence or act like you know everything. You just need to stop apologizing for your presence.

Belonging starts with belief. Not believing that everything will go perfectly, but believing that you deserve to show up and take up space, regardless of outcome. You may get things wrong. You may feel awkward. You may not get the response you hope for. That's okay. Belonging isn't about controlling the outcome it's about committing to show up as your whole self, even when the outcome is uncertain.

Confidence grows when you do the thing *while* feeling unsure. It grows when you stop waiting to feel 100% ready before walking into a room or speaking your mind. It grows when you remind yourself that you are not a guest in your own life you are the host of your experience. That's not something you earn later. That's something you step into now.

If your mind tries to tell you, "You're not qualified," or "They're going to judge you," try asking a better question: "What if I belong here just as I am?" Let that question sit for a moment. What if you already have everything you need to be in this space not because you're perfect, but because you're human?

Here's something else to remember: people are usually too busy thinking about themselves to judge you the way you imagine. While you're worrying about what others think of your outfit, your voice, and your ideas, they're often wondering the same things about themselves. We all want to be accepted. We all want to be respected. But that begins with respecting ourselves first.

Walking into a space like you belong doesn't mean you'll never feel nervous again. It simply means you won't let nervousness hold you back. You'll walk in anyway. You'll speak up anyway. You'll stand in your own energy without apology. And with every time you do that, your confidence grows.

The goal isn't to fake confidence. The goal is to practice showing up, over and over, until it starts to feel more natural. You'll still have doubts sometimes. But doubt doesn't disqualify you. It just means you're doing something that matters.

Let this be your reminder today: You don't need to earn your place in the room. You *already* belong. You don't have to prove yourself by being the loudest, the smartest, or the most polished. Just be present. Be honest. And let that be enough.

5-Minute Practice: Walk Like You Belong

Choose one space today to walk into with intention. It might be a meeting, a store, a classroom, or a simple conversation.

Before you enter:

- Pause for one deep breath.
- Check your posture keep your head up and shoulders back.
- Silently say to yourself: "I belong here."

As you enter:

- Don't rush to shrink or disappear. Let yourself take up space.

- Make eye contact if you feel comfortable. Let your presence be felt.
- Speak if you want to. Or just be still but be present.

This may feel uncomfortable at first. But discomfort doesn't mean you're doing it wrong. It means you're growing.

Repeat This Thought Today:

"I belong in every space I enter. I don't have to shrink to fit."

Every time you say it, you make it a little truer. Keep practicing. You're already becoming the version of you who walks in with quiet confidence. Let the room adjust to *you*.

DAY 20: THE CONFIDENCE OF SAYING NO

Saying "no" sounds simple. It's just two letters. A short word. But for many people, it feels heavy. Like you're doing something wrong. Saying no can often come with feelings of guilt, fear, and second-guessing. You might worry that you'll upset someone, that they'll think you're selfish or unkind. Maybe you've spent most of your life trying to be helpful, agreeable, or easygoing and saying no doesn't fit with how you've been taught to behave.

But here's the truth: confidence is not just about saying yes to opportunity. It's also about knowing when to say no. Real confidence means knowing your limits, honoring your values, and protecting your time and energy. When you say no to something that doesn't feel right for you, you're actually saying yes to yourself. That is not selfish it's self-respect.

Most people who struggle to say no are not weak or uncertain. They're often strong and deeply caring. They want to help, to be kind, to show up for others. But that care can turn into over commitment. You end up stretched too thin, overwhelmed, or even resentful. And the more you keep saying yes when you really want to say no, the more your confidence starts to shrink.

Think about the last time you said yes even though you didn't want to. Maybe it was a request to help out when you were already too busy. Maybe it was agreeing to plans when you were exhausted. Maybe it was staying quiet when you disagreed with something. Afterward, you probably didn't feel proud or happy you might have felt frustrated, depleted, or invisible.

That's the cost of not saying no. When you ignore your own needs to keep others comfortable, you slowly lose trust in yourself. And confidence needs self-trust to grow.

Of course, there are times when we all have to do things we'd rather not do such as responsibilities, favors, or moments of compromise. However, there's a significant difference between choosing to help and feeling obligated to do so. One comes from strength. The other comes from fear.

Learning to say no with confidence doesn't mean you become rude or cold. It means you learn to speak up with clarity and kindness. You learn to check in with yourself first, instead of defaulting to people-pleasing. With practice, it begins to feel more natural.

Here's something important: saying no doesn't always need a long explanation. You don't have to list ten reasons or over-apologize. "I can't right now" or "That doesn't work for me" is enough. Your no is valid, even when it's simple.

You also don't need to wait until you're completely sure or confident to say it. Sometimes, your voice might shake. Sometimes, you'll feel awkward. That's okay. It doesn't mean you're doing it wrong. It means you're growing.

Try this practice:

Before responding to a request, pause. Ask yourself a few honest questions:

- Do I want to do this?
- Do I have the time and energy for this?
- Am I saying yes because I feel guilty or afraid to say no?

That moment of pause gives you space to respond from choice, not pressure.

Now let's look at a few simple ways to say no with confidence:

1. "Thanks for thinking of me, but I'm not available."

This is polite and clear. You're expressing appreciation without taking on something that doesn't fit.

2. "I can't take that on right now."

This is direct and doesn't invite negotiation. You're letting someone know your plate is full without over-explaining.

3. "That's not something I can commit to, but I hope it goes well."

This keeps the tone supportive while still holding your boundary.

4. "I'm not the right person for that."

This is helpful when someone expects you to do something outside your role or comfort zone.

5. "No, thank you."

Sometimes, the simplest answer is the strongest.

The more you use phrases like these, the easier it becomes to stand in your own. And as you start doing it more often, you'll notice a shift. You'll feel more in control of your time. You'll stop dreading requests. You'll begin to feel proud of the moments you chose honesty over obligation.

It's also worth noting that not everyone will like your no. Some people might push back. They might be used to you saying yes, and your new boundaries may surprise them. That's okay. Their reaction isn't your responsibility. You are not in charge of other people's comfort you're in charge of your own truth.

It helps to remind yourself: people who respect you will respect your no. If someone gets angry or distant because you've honored your own limits, that says more about them than it does about you.

Sometimes, saying no is about small things. Declining an invitation. Saying you can't take on one more task. At other times, it's about making bigger decisions such as ending a draining relationship, walking away from a project, or turning down an opportunity that doesn't align with your values. In both cases, the skill is the same: listening to yourself first, then speaking from that place.

There's also a quiet strength that comes from not over-apologizing when you say no. You are allowed to disappoint people. You are allowed to prioritize your well-being. That doesn't make you difficult or unkind. It makes you someone who takes responsibility for their life.

Think of your no as a door. When you close one door that doesn't serve you, you open another door to rest, creativity, clarity, or a yes that really matters. Every no clears space for a better yes.

Here's a journal prompt to explore today:

What's one time I said yes when I wanted to say no? What did I feel afterward? What would I say next time instead?

Write it down. Practice the new response out loud if you want. Rehearsing helps it feel less scary in real life.

Here's another reflection:

Where in my life am I afraid to say no? What do I fear will happen if I do? What could happen instead?

This helps you notice the stories fear tells you and begin to challenge them.

Repeat this phrase to yourself throughout the day:

"Saying no is not rejection. It's direction."

Let that remind you: every time you say no, you're choosing a clearer path for yourself. You're building self-trust. You're making space for what matters most.

Confidence doesn't mean you never doubt. It means you act from respect instead of fear. And learning to say no is one of the most respectful things you can do for yourself, and for the life you're building.

So today, practice your no. Even if it's small. Even if it's awkward. Even if your voice shakes. That's not a weakness. That's courage.

You're learning that your needs matter. Your time is important. Your energy is not endless.

You don't owe everyone a yes.

What you owe yourself is the truth. Keep telling it. One at a time.

DAY 21: STOP OVER-APOLOGIZING

How often do you catch yourself saying "sorry"? Not just when you've actually done something wrong, but when you've simply taken up space, asked a question, or expressed a need? Maybe you've apologized for asking for help, for speaking your mind, for being late by one minute, or for something completely outside your control. It might feel like a habit, something small and harmless but over time, over-apologizing can quietly erode your confidence.

The truth is, many people especially those who were taught to be polite, accommodating, or "easy to be around" learned to apologize for everything. It's not always about guilt. Often, it's about fear: fear of being seen as too much, fear of causing conflict, fear of being judged or rejected. When you over-apologize, what you're really saying is, "I'm sorry for existing in a way that might make someone uncomfortable." And that's a painful weight to carry.

Confidence means you stop apologizing for things that don't require an apology. It means you stop saying 'sorry' when you're not truly sorry. You don't have to apologize for having needs, for setting boundaries, for speaking up, for asking questions, or for being yourself. You're allowed to take up space without guilt.

It's important to understand that being polite and being apologetic isn't the same thing. Politeness comes from respect. Over-apologizing often comes from insecurity. One builds a connection. The other slowly tears down your self-worth. And the more you apologize unnecessarily, the more you send the message to yourself and others that your presence is a problem to fix.

Let's look at what over-apologizing can sound like:

- "Sorry, could I just say something?"
- "I'm sorry, I just thought..."
- "Sorry for bothering you."
- "Sorry, this might be a dumb question, but..."
- "Sorry, I'm not making sense."

None of these statements is "bad." But if you're using them regularly, it might be time to ask yourself why. Are you apologizing because you genuinely regret something? Or are you apologizing because you feel unsure, unworthy, or like you're not allowed to speak freely?

There's a big difference between a real apology and an automatic one. A genuine apology comes from taking responsibility for something you've done wrong such as hurting someone or breaking a promise. That kind of apology matters. But if you're apologizing just for being in the room, having a voice, or taking time to think, that's not an apology it's a habit rooted in doubt.

Here's what happens when you start breaking that habit: you begin to hear your own voice more clearly. You build self-trust. You feel stronger and more grounded in your choices. And other people notice, too. When you speak without apology, you're easier to hear. Your words carry more weight. You show others how you expect to be treated.

One helpful shift is to replace "sorry" with "thank you." Instead of saying, "Sorry I'm late," try, "Thank you for waiting." Instead of "Sorry for the confusion," try "Thanks for your patience while I figured that out." This small change moves your words from self-blame to gratitude. It's respectful, but not self-erasing.

Let's take a closer look at a few examples and how you might rephrase them:

Instead of: "Sorry for asking so many questions."

Try: "Thank you for helping me understand."

Instead of: "Sorry, I need a minute to think."

Try: "Give me a second to gather my thoughts."

Instead of: "Sorry if I'm being annoying."

Try: "I appreciate you listening."

Instead of: "Sorry, I can't take that on."

Try: "I'm not available for that right now."

These alternatives are simple but powerful. They help you stay grounded in your values, even when you're making a request or setting a boundary.

If this shift feels hard, you're not alone. Over-apologizing is often something we learn early in life. Maybe you were told to be polite above all else. Perhaps you were raised in a family or culture where disagreement was perceived as a sign of disrespect. Maybe you learned that keeping the peace meant staying small. It makes sense that your words reflect those lessons. But just because you learned something doesn't mean you can't unlearn it.

One way to start changing this pattern is to pause when you feel the urge to say sorry. Ask yourself:

- Did I actually do something wrong?
- Is there a more effective way to convey what I need to say?
- Am I saying sorry just to make someone else more comfortable?

These questions aren't meant to shame you. They're meant to wake you up to how often you give your power away without realizing it. The goal isn't to stop saying sorry altogether it's to save your apologies for the moments that really matter.

Try this 5-minute confidence practice today:

Step 1: Write down three situations from the past week where you apologized unnecessarily.

Step 2: Rewrite each statement using more confident language something clear, respectful, and unapologetic.

Step 3: Say the new versions out loud. Even if it feels awkward at first, practicing out loud helps your brain create a new pattern.

Step 4: Pay attention throughout the day. When you catch yourself starting to say "sorry," pause and try something different. Even if it's just a small change, it counts.

Let today be the day you stop apologizing for being who you are.

You don't need to say sorry for:

- Needing time
- Having boundaries
- Taking care of yourself

- Asking for clarity
- Taking up space
- Saying "no"

Confidence doesn't come from never making mistakes. It comes from standing in your truth without shrinking. From knowing you matter, choose your words instead of apologizing for them.

Here's a reminder to repeat throughout your day:

"I don't have to apologize for being here. My presence is not a problem."

Say it often. Say it when you feel unsure. Say it when the old habit creeps in.

And if someone does expect you to apologize for simply existing, ask yourself if that's someone you need to keep pleasing.

Confidence doesn't mean being loud or perfect. Sometimes, it's as quiet as not saying sorry. Sometimes, it's as simple as choosing to speak like your words have weight because they do.

You are allowed to be heard. You are allowed to take your time. You are allowed to show up fully, without needing to explain away your existence.

So the next time you feel the urge to apologize, pause. Breathe. Choose trust instead of fear. Replace the apology with something honest and kind.

You're not being rude. You're just learning to speak from a place of self-respect.

And that shift? It changes everything. One word at a time.

WEEK 4: KEEP SHOWING UP FOR YOURSELF

Theme: Turning confidence into your new normal

By now, you've done some meaningful work. You've started shifting your thoughts, changed the way you speak to yourself, and taken small but powerful actions in the real world. This final week is about something just as important: consistency. It's about turning everything you've practiced into your new normal not a performance, not a temporary boost, but a steady way of being.

Confidence isn't a moment. It's not a perfect outfit or a single brave conversation. It's something you build through repetition. Every time you speak up, every time you stop apologizing unnecessarily, every time you act with honesty and self-respect, you are reinforcing a new identity. You're becoming someone who trusts themselves, someone who doesn't abandon their needs, and someone who keeps showing up.

The truth is, confidence is not about never having self-doubt. It's about what you do with those doubts when they show up. Do you let them shut you down, or do you notice them, pause, and choose to keep going anyway? That's the work of this week: to keep going. To keep choosing your voice, your needs, your truth even when it would be easier to fall back into old habits.

You don't need to be perfect to be consistent. Some days you'll feel strong and clear. Other days you'll feel unsure or tired. But showing up for yourself doesn't mean doing everything perfectly it means you don't leave yourself behind. You honor your needs, even in small ways. You protect your time. You rest when needed. You speak kindly to yourself. You keep practicing.

Confidence grows when you treat yourself like someone worth sticking with. If a friend made a mistake, you wouldn't call them a failure. You'd encourage them. You'd remind them of their progress. That's the kind of relationship you're building with yourself now one of patience, trust, and care.

This week, we'll focus on how to turn your confidence into a steady habit. You'll reflect on how far you've come, look for proof of your growth, and keep building simple routines that help you stay connected to your strength. You'll also explore how to show up when no one else is cheering you on because that's when real self-trust is formed.

You're not going back to who you were. You're not pretending to be someone you're not. You're staying with the person you're becoming. You're proving, day by day, that confidence isn't something you wait for it's something you choose, over and over again.

Keep showing up. Even when it's quiet. Even when it's messy. Even when no one sees it but you.

That's how confidence becomes real. That's how it becomes yours.

DAY 22: LET GO OF IMPRESSING OTHERS

TRYING to impress other people can feel like a full-time job. You might find yourself editing your words, second-guessing your choices, or adjusting your behavior just to seem more likable, intelligent, successful, or "put together." Sometimes, it doesn't even feel like you're doing it on purpose it becomes automatic. But this constant performance is exhausting, and it slowly pulls you away from who you really are.

The need to impress others often begins at a young age. You may have discovered that you received more praise when you were helpful, quiet, or easy to be around. Or that making people laugh, staying agreeable, or achieving certain things won you attention. Over time, you started measuring your value by how people responded to you. But here's the truth: real confidence isn't built on performance. It's built on being able to like yourself when no one else is watching, approving, or applauding.

Letting go of impressing others doesn't mean you stop caring about people or how you treat them. It means you stop molding yourself to fit their expectations. It means you no longer trade in your own peace, needs, or truth just to win approval. When you live to impress, you begin to perform instead of living. Your choices become about what looks good, not what feels right. You might dress in a way that fits in, but it doesn't reflect who you are. You might stay quiet when you want to speak. You might accept situations that don't serve you, just to avoid being seen as "difficult."

This daily shape-shifting creates distance between you and your real self. Over time, it becomes harder to know what you actually want, what you actually believe, or how you actually feel. Your confidence weakens not because you aren't strong, but because you've been looking outward for something that can only be built inside.

So, what happens when you stop trying to impress? At first, it can feel scary. You might worry people will judge you or walk away. You might fear being misunderstood or seen differently. But as you keep showing up honestly, you'll notice something important: the right people stay. And the ones who were only impressed by the version of you that wasn't real? They were never really seeing you anyway.

You begin to reclaim your time, your energy, and your voice. You dress in what makes you feel strong, not what's "on trend." You speak up even when your opinion differs from others. You ask for what you need without wrapping it in apology or performance. You no longer need every room to love you. You become more grounded in your own approval, your own truth, and your own pace.

Confidence isn't loud. It's steady. It says, "This is who I am. Not for show. Not for attention. Just for me." You don't have to prove yourself every moment. You don't need to sparkle constantly. You are not a brand, a product, or a campaign. You're a real person with real needs, real thoughts, and real worth.

Think about how much mental space is freed up when you stop performing. Think about what you could do, create, or say if you weren't worrying about how others would react. That space is yours to reclaim. It starts when you shift your focus from how you're being seen to how you actually feel.

Ask yourself: "Am I doing this because it feels right to me? Or am I doing this to be liked?" When you feel torn between choices, try choosing the one that aligns with your values not just the one that brings approval. When you're tempted to polish yourself to please others, ask, "What would I choose if no one else had an opinion?"

Letting go of impressing people doesn't mean being unkind or careless. It means being real. It means respecting others without abandoning yourself. It means understanding that not everyone will get you and that's not a problem you need to fix. It's part of being a person with your own voice and rhythm.

The most magnetic people aren't those who chase attention. They're the ones who are comfortable in their own skin. They don't need to explain themselves or force anyone to see their worth. They show up as they are, and let the rest fall into place.

This shift is a practice. Some days you'll catch yourself trying to impress. That's okay. Don't shame yourself. Just notice it. Take a breath. And ask yourself what honesty would look like instead. Perhaps it means saying no when you truly want to. Maybe it means not over-explaining yourself. Maybe it means posting something online without perfect lighting or filters. Maybe it means admitting you don't know something, instead of pretending you do.

One small choice at a time, you teach your brain that being real is safe. And little by little, confidence grows.

Try this today: Before making a decision, pause and ask, "If I weren't trying to impress anyone, what would I do?" Write that answer down. Even if you don't act on it yet, just knowing your truth is powerful. You're allowed to choose what feels right to you even if it's different, even if it's not popular, even if no one claps.

You don't have to live on a stage. You don't have to polish every sentence, perfect every moment, or win everyone's approval. You just have to keep coming back to your voice, your values, and your real self.

And that version of you the one who shows up without a mask is more than enough.

Daily Thought:

I don't need to impress others to prove my worth. My truth is enough.

Today's Practice:

Choose one small action that's for you not for impressing anyone else. Maybe it's wearing what you really like. Saying no without over-explaining. Sharing your real opinion. Or doing something you love without worrying what others think. Let that be your practice today.

Keep Going:

Every time you choose honesty over performance, your confidence strengthens. You start to build a life that fits who you are not just who you think others want you to be. That's freedom. That's peace. And that's real strength. Keep showing up for that version of you. They're worth it.

DAY 23: FINDING SAFETY WITHOUT HIDING

When we think of safety, we often associate it with comfort, quiet, or escape. For many people, safety has become tied to hiding staying silent, keeping your head down, avoiding attention, or making yourself smaller. You might feel safest when no one is looking at you, questioning you, or expecting too much from you. And that feeling is understandable. Hiding can feel like protection, especially if you've been hurt, rejected, judged, or misunderstood in the past.

But here's the hard truth: while hiding may feel safe, it also keeps you stuck. It keeps you from being fully seen, heard, and known not just by others, but by yourself as well. When you hide too much, you start to forget what it feels like to stand in your own presence. You begin to shrink your goals, silence your voice, and disconnect from your real self. And you might not even notice it happening, because hiding has become second nature.

Maybe you learned to hide in small ways by laughing off your ideas, pretending you didn't care, or brushing off compliments. Maybe you told yourself, "It's not that important," or "It's better not to say anything." Over time, those habits form a pattern, and the pattern becomes your comfort zone. The problem is that the zone might be comfortable, but it's not where growth lives.

You don't need to live in fear to stay safe. There is a difference between protection and limitation. Safety should mean being able to exist fully without being punished for it. It should mean being able to speak, try, express, and exist without hiding who you are. But when fear leads, we trade real safety for false control. We think, "If I just stay small, I won't get hurt." And that belief can rule your life if you're not careful.

So, how do you find safety without losing it? It begins by slowly rebuilding trust in yourself. Not in a dramatic, show-everything-all-at-once kind of way but in quiet, steady moments where you let yourself be seen, little by little. It starts with acknowledging that you're allowed to take up space, even if you've been told otherwise. It starts with recognizing when you're hiding not to judge yourself, but to ask, "Do I still need to do this? Or is there room to show more of me now?"

You might not feel ready to go all in. That's okay. Confidence doesn't ask you to jump off a cliff. It simply asks you to take one small step outside your comfort zone. That might look like speaking up in a meeting, showing emotion when you usually hide it, or simply sharing your honest opinion in a safe place. Each of those acts is a brick in building a new version of safety one that includes your voice, not just your silence.

Many people think being seen makes them more vulnerable to pain. And yes, vulnerability can open you up to discomfort but it also opens the door to connection, truth, and freedom. When you show up as your full self, you invite the world to meet you where you truly are not behind a mask or a performance, but in your authenticity.

This doesn't mean trusting everyone. It means trusting yourself to know when and where to be seen. It means knowing that even if someone misunderstands you or doesn't like what you say, you'll still be okay. It means knowing that your worth isn't based on how perfectly you protect yourself but on how deeply you show up for yourself.

Think about the last time you held back, not because you didn't want to speak, but because it felt safer not to. What did that moment cost you? Maybe it cost you an opportunity, a real conversation, or a chance to express your ideas. Now imagine what might have happened if you had shown up a little more what connection you could have created, what self-trust you could have built.

When you practice finding safety without hiding, you build inner strength. You begin to believe that you can face discomfort without running from it. You start to create your own definition of safety one that doesn't depend on disappearing, but on being grounded in who you are. That's real security: knowing that no matter what happens, you are not betraying yourself.

To help you shift, start noticing the moments when you begin to shrink. Do your shoulders drop? Does your voice get quieter? Do you immediately try to please or blend in? These are signs your brain is trying to protect you in old ways. You can gently interrupt that pattern by saying, "It's okay to be here. I don't need to hide." Even that small phrase can make a difference. It helps your nervous system feel supported, not abandoned.

You don't need to go from invisible to spotlight overnight. You just need to be honest about how much of yourself you've been keeping hidden, and ask what you're ready to bring forward. Maybe it's your humor. Your opinions. Your creativity. Your boundaries. Your grief. Your dreams. You get to choose. And every time you decide to be more of yourself, you find safety rooted in truth not fear.

Try this today: choose one moment where you usually hide, and instead, let yourself be seen in a small way. That might mean making eye contact, using your real voice instead of a softer version, or sharing a real answer when someone asks how you're doing. Let that moment remind you: safety and hiding don't have to go together anymore.

Daily Reminder:

"I am safe to show up as myself. I don't have to hide to be okay."

Practice Prompt:

Think of a moment today when you chose to hide, even just a little. What would it have felt like to stay present instead? What's one small thing you can try tomorrow that helps you build safety from within without disappearing?

Keep Going:

The more you choose truth over hiding, the more grounded you'll feel. You'll stop needing approval to feel safe. You'll stop looking for escape when things feel hard. You'll start showing up in your life with a quiet strength that says, "I belong here. Even if I'm scared. Even if I'm unsure. I don't have to vanish to feel okay."

You're not here to vanish. You're here to live and you can do that with your whole self, one honest moment at a time.

DAY 24: THE POWER OF "I DON'T KNOW YET"

CONFIDENCE OFTEN GETS MISTAKEN for having all the answers. People tend to associate being sure of yourself with being completely certain knowing what to say, what to do, and how to do it at all times. But real confidence isn't about having everything figured out. It's about how you respond when you don't. And one of the most powerful, honest things you can say is: "I don't know yet."

Those three little words carry more strength than most people realize. Saying "I don't know yet" doesn't mean you're weak, unprepared, or falling behind. It means you're open. It means you're still learning. It means you're strong enough to admit you don't have the answer and steady enough not to fake it.

Too many people feel like admitting they don't know something is a failure. Maybe you were taught that asking questions made you look less smart, or that uncertainty meant you weren't capable. So you stayed quiet. You guessed instead of asking. Or you pretended you understood when you didn't. All of that builds a fear-based version of confidence one that's based on keeping up appearances, not telling the truth.

But when you allow yourself to say "I don't know yet," you take your power back. You stop pretending. You stop trying to impress. You let yourself be real. And being real is where confidence actually grows. Real confidence isn't built on being right all the time it's built on being willing to grow without shame.

Adding the word "yet" is especially important. Without it, "I don't know" can feel final. Like you've hit a wall or admitted defeat. But "I don't know yet" leaves the door open. It says: I'm still in progress. I'm capable of learning. I haven't figured it out but I can, and I will. That's a mindset shift that fosters self-respect rather than self-judgment.

Think about how different that feels. Instead of saying "I'm bad at this," you say, "I haven't learned this yet." Instead of saying, "I don't get it," you say, "I'm still figuring it out." Instead of shutting yourself down with fear or shame, you offer yourself space to grow. That's where learning thrives. That's where curiosity comes back. That's where your confidence becomes strong and flexible not brittle and afraid of mistakes.

This mindset benefits many areas of life. At work, it gives you permission to ask questions instead of faking expertise. In relationships, it helps you express when you're unsure or still figuring out your needs. In learning encourages progress instead of pressure. And in self-talk, it changes the story from "I'm not enough" to "I'm still growing."

Here's the thing: nobody knows everything. Even experts. Even people who seem confident. Everyone is learning something. Everyone is uncertain sometimes. The difference lies in whether some people let it be a source of shame, while others view it as a space for growth.

"I don't know yet" is a skill. And like any skill, it gets easier with practice. At first, it might feel uncomfortable. You might feel exposed. But over time, it becomes freeing. You no longer have to perform. You no longer have to pretend. You get to be where you are honestly, fully, and without apology.

Let's also discuss how this phrase can impact your relationships with others. When you admit you don't know yet, you create space for genuine conversation. People around you feel safer to accept their own learning process, too. It lowers the pressure in the room. It encourages curiosity, collaboration, and honesty.

It also builds trust. Because people can feel when you're faking certainty. They may not say anything, but it creates tension. When you own your learning curve, people often respect you more not less. It demonstrates humility, but also courage.

Here are some examples of how "I don't know yet" might show up in your daily life:

- In a meeting, instead of nodding and pretending you understand something, you might say, "I'm not familiar with that yet. Could you explain it a bit more?"
- When someone asks you a question you're unsure about, you might respond, "I don't know yet, but I'll find out and get back to you."
- If you're struggling with a task, instead of saying, "I'm just bad at this," try saying, "I'm still learning how to do this well."
- When reflecting on your personal goals, you might say, "I'm not sure exactly what I want yet, but I'm exploring it."

Every time you use this phrase, you give yourself permission to grow. You give yourself space to breathe. You stop expecting perfection, and you start allowing the process. That shift makes all the difference.

You can even apply this mindset to your inner critic. The next time you hear that voice saying, "You should already know how to do this," respond with, "I don't know yet but I'm learning." That's how you begin to cultivate a distinct inner voice. One that's not harsh or punishing, but honest and kind.

Confidence doesn't mean having all the answers. It means trusting yourself enough to not fake it. It means believing in your ability to figure things out. It means standing in the space between "I don't know" and "I will."

Here's a simple practice:

Think of one area of your life where you've been avoiding action because you don't feel ready. Maybe it's a conversation, a project, or a personal goal. Write down this sentence:

"I don't know how to _____ yet."

Then underneath, write:

"But I'm willing to learn."

Look at that sentence every time you feel stuck. Say it out loud if you can. Let yourself feel how different that sounds from "I can't." One creates a wall. The other opens a door.

You can also reflect on times in your past when you didn't know something and then learned. Remind yourself that this is part of your process. You've figured things out before. You will again.

Daily Reminder:

"I don't need all the answers. I need curiosity and courage. I'm still learning, and that's enough."

Keep Going:

Every time you let go of the need to be perfect and choose honesty instead, your confidence grows. Not because you're flawless but because you're real. You're learning how to stand strong in the middle of uncertainty. You're building trust with yourself. You're letting "I don't know yet" be a bridge instead of a wall.

You are not falling behind. You're becoming. One question, one step, and one honest moment at a time. Keep going. Keep learning. You're right on time.

DAY 25: KEEPING PROMISES TO YOURSELF

Confidence isn't just about how you speak or how you stand. It's also about what you do when no one is watching especially when it comes to the promises you make to yourself. Every time you say, "I'll do this," and then follow through, you send a message to yourself that your word matters. Not just to others, but to you as well. That quiet, inner sense of self-trust? That's one of the most powerful foundations for real, lasting confidence.

Keeping promises to yourself might sound simple, but it's not always easy. Life gets busy. You get tired. Doubt creeps in. Suddenly, the thing you promised yourself whether it's starting a project, taking more rest, saying no, or speaking up gets pushed aside. And while that might feel harmless in the moment, something subtle begins to shift. Each time you break a promise to yourself, even a small one, it chips away at your self-trust. You might not notice right away, but over time, it adds up. You start to believe that your own word can't be counted on. That you can't be counted on. And that hurts your confidence more than any outside opinion ever could.

The good news? You can rebuild that trust one kept promise at a time.

Think about how much effort many of us put into being reliable for others. We show up for work, return calls, keep appointments, and help out when asked. Why? Because we want to be dependable. We want others to feel they can count on us. But do you show yourself to be that reliable? If you say you're going to rest, do you actually rest? If you say you're going to stop working at 6 PM, do you close the laptop or just push a little more? If you say you're going to start that goal, do you start or do you keep moving the date?

The truth is, many of us are great at keeping promises to others and terrible at keeping them to ourselves. And it's not because we're lazy or unmotivated. Often, it's because we've been taught that our needs come last. That showing up for others is what matters most. That we're selfish if we draw boundaries. However, the more you delay or abandon your own needs, the weaker your sense of self-trust becomes. And without self-trust, confidence can't grow.

So, what counts as a promise to yourself? It doesn't have to be something huge or dramatic. It could be:

- I'll speak up in that meeting.
- I'll stretch for 5 minutes each morning.
- I won't check my phone first thing tomorrow.
- I'll take a break instead of pushing through burnout.
- I'll stop apologizing for things that don't need apologies.
- I'll go to bed earlier tonight.
- I'll say what I mean instead of sugarcoating it.

These are small promises, but they matter. Every one you keep builds a little more self-trust. And over time, that trust turns into belief the quiet belief that you can count on yourself no matter what.

The key to keeping promises to yourself is to start small and make them specific. Vague promises like "I'll take better care of myself" or "I'll be more confident" are hard to act on. They don't tell your brain what to actually do. Instead, try making your promise something clear and doable: "I'll take a 10-minute walk today." "I'll say no to that thing I don't want to do." "I'll drink a glass of water before I reach for coffee." When your promise is simple and straightforward, it's easier to follow through. And when you follow through, your trust grows stronger.

And here's the other part: You don't have to be perfect. Missing one promise doesn't mean you've failed. What matters is what you do next. Do you shame yourself and give up? Or do you get curious and come back to the promise with compassion? Self-trust isn't built on never messing up. It's built on what you do when you mess up.

Let's say you promised yourself you'd go for a short walk after work. But the day got hectic, and you forgot. You could say, "See? I can never stick to anything," and give up. Or you could say, "Okay, I missed it today but I still want to show up for myself. I'll try again tomorrow." That second choice? That's what builds trust. That's what builds confidence. Not the flawless execution, but the steady, honest return.

Another helpful shift is treating your self-promises like commitments you've made to someone you deeply respect. Imagine if a close friend made a plan with you and kept cancelling. Over time, you'd stop trusting them. You'd stop depending on their word. That's exactly what happens when you make and break promises to yourself. But flip it around. If someone consistently followed through, you'd feel safe with them. You'd trust their word. That's the energy you're building with yourself when you show up like someone who matters.

There's also something healing about keeping promises in areas where you've been hurt or doubted in the past. Maybe someone once told you that you weren't consistent, that you never followed through. Maybe you internalized that, and now it feels true. But it's not. You're allowed to rewrite that story. You're allowed to become someone who follows through. Even if it's one small promise at a time.

Here's a simple practice to try today:

Write down one promise you want to make to yourself. Keep it simple. Keep it doable. Something that takes less than 10 minutes. Then do it on purpose. Don't let it be accidental. Keep it like it matters. Then notice how you feel afterward. Not just proud, but safer with yourself. More stable. More grounded.

You can even build this into your daily routine. At the start of each day, write one promise. One action that says, "I'm listening to myself." "I matter." "My word means something." These aren't just tasks they're signals to your brain that you're someone who shows up.

Remember: the goal is not perfection. The goal is consistency, over time, with compassion. Life will get busy. Things will come up. You'll forget. However, that doesn't mean you're back at square one. It means you get to practice returning. Over and over, building self-trust one choice at a time.

Daily Reminder:

"My promises to myself matter. I trust my word. I keep showing up even when it's hard."

Keep Going:

Confidence isn't loud. It's steady. It's the quiet, repeated belief that you can count on yourself. That your voice matters. That your actions match your values. And the more you keep the promises you make to yourself, the more you'll walk through life with that kind of quiet confidence. You don't need anyone else's permission. You don't need to prove anything. Just stay true to your word and watch your confidence grow.

DAY 26: FEELING CONFIDENT VS. LOOKING CONFIDENT

It's easy to think confidence is something you either have or don't. That it's something you can see right away in someone the way they walk into a room, speak without hesitation, or lead a conversation. But the truth is, what confidence looks like on the outside and what it feels like on the inside are often very different. And chasing the image of confidence without building the feeling can leave you feeling more disconnected than before.

Looking confident is about appearance. Feeling confident is about self-trust. One is for others to see. The other is for you to live. And the difference matters.

Let's talk about what it means to "look" confident. This can show up in ways like:

- Standing up straight
- Making eye contact
- Speaking clearly
- Taking the lead in a group
- Smiling, even when you feel nervous

- Being the one who seems "put together"

There's nothing wrong with these things. In fact, many of them can be helpful habits. They can support your presence and help you feel more grounded in certain situations. But here's where it gets tricky: sometimes people get stuck trying to *perform* confidence instead of actually *building* it.

If you're only focused on looking confident, you might end up ignoring what's really happening inside. You might hide your fear, silence your doubt, and pretend everything is fine even when it's not. Over time, this can create a gap between how you feel and how you act. That gap can make you feel like a fake, even when you're doing everything "right."

Confidence doesn't mean never feeling nervous. It doesn't mean never having doubts. It means being able to notice those feelings and still choose to move forward. It means knowing that you don't have to hide your humanity to be taken seriously.

Real confidence starts with honesty. It begins with accepting yourself your voice, your pace, your way of doing things. It doesn't demand perfection or a flawless image. It grows when you treat yourself with respect, when you keep your promises, and when you stop judging yourself for having normal human emotions.

Have you ever met someone who looked confident but didn't feel trustworthy? Perhaps they were loud, charming, or always had something to say but there was something about their energy that felt off. That's what happens when someone tries to look confident without actually *being* in alignment with themselves. It's a performance. And it wears people out including the person doing the performing.

On the other hand, you've probably also met someone who didn't speak much, but when they did, you listened. Someone who seemed calm, grounded, and clear even if they weren't the loudest in the room. That's what feeling confident looks like. It's not about grabbing attention. It's about being rooted in yourself.

Feeling confident is quiet. Steady. It comes from self-awareness, not showmanship. It means you're not trying to impress everyone. You're not chasing approval. You're simply living from a place of self-respect and trust. You know who you are, even if you're still figuring things out.

That kind of confidence doesn't need to be loud to be real.

Of course, there's nothing wrong with using body language and speech tools to support yourself. Practicing standing tall, breathing deeply, or speaking clearly can help calm your nervous system. Those are tools not lies. The problem only comes when you use the image of confidence to cover up the work you still need to do inside.

So, how do you know if you're *feeling* confident instead of just *trying* to look confident? Here are a few signs:

- You can admit when you don't know something, without shame.
- You let yourself be seen, even when you're unsure.
- You speak honestly, not just in ways that will win approval.
- You know your strengths, and you also know your limits and neither makes you any less worthy.
- You're okay with silence or not having all the answers.
- You don't feel the need to prove yourself all the time.

You also stop obsessing over how others perceive you. When you feel confident, your attention isn't constantly bouncing between yourself and the imagined thoughts of other people. You stay more present. You stay more in your own energy. That's when your confidence feels real not performative.

This doesn't mean you won't still care about how you show up. It's natural to want to make a good impression or to feel polished in important moments. But when your focus is rooted in self-respect instead of fear of rejection, the pressure softens. You can take feedback without falling apart. You can hear a "no" without questioning your entire worth. You can show up, try, and even fail without losing yourself.

Here's something helpful to ask yourself: "Am I doing this to connect, or am I doing this to impress?" Connection is a sign of internal confidence. Impressing others is often a sign that you're trying to borrow confidence from outside approval. When you start shifting from performance to connection, you'll feel the difference in your body. There's less tension. Less self-monitoring. More space to be real.

That kind of shift takes time. It comes with practice. It comes with noticing when you're in performance mode and gently reminding yourself that it's safe to come back to who you are. It comes with not punishing yourself for feeling nervous or uncertain.

You're not supposed to be confident *all the time*. No one is. What you can be is honest with yourself about what you're feeling and still choose to act in a way that supports your values.

Here's a small practice to try today:

Pick a moment where you'd normally try to "look" confident. Maybe it's in a meeting, a conversation, or a post you want to share. Instead of asking, "How do I come across?" ask, "What feels honest to me right now?" Say or do the thing that's real, even if it's a little less polished. Then notice how it feels. Notice if something inside you softens.

That softness? That's your nervous system starting to feel safer in your truth.

You don't need to "look" confident to be confident. And you don't need to perform to be taken seriously. The more you trust yourself to show up as you are, the more your presence will speak for itself. Not because you're loud. Not because you're perfect. But because you're steady. Grounded. Real.

That's what people actually respond to. Not a perfect image but a grounded person who trusts their own voice enough to speak without pretending.

Daily Thought:

"I don't need to look confident to be confident. I'm allowed to show up as I am."

Keep Going:

Each day you stop performing and start practicing self-trust, your confidence grows. It's not about getting louder. It's about getting more honest with yourself, and with the world. And when that happens, people don't just see confidence they feel it. So do you.

DAY 27: CONFIDENCE IS PRACTICE, NOT PERFECTION

CONFIDENCE OFTEN GETS MISTAKEN for something final. People imagine it as a fixed quality you either have or don't. They think confident people were just born that way, or they had one big success and now they never doubt themselves again. But that's not how confidence works.

Real confidence isn't about being perfect. It's about the power of practice, the ability to keep going even when it's hard. This is where your control lies, especially when it's hard.

Confidence is built through small actions, not big moments. It's not something you achieve and then get to keep forever. It's something you grow into by showing up, trying again, and giving yourself permission to be imperfect while still moving forward. That's what practice is: the space where progress happens, even when it's messy.

Consider how you learn new things whether it's riding a bike, learning to cook, or speaking in public. You probably weren't great the first time. You probably messed up, stumbled, second-guessed, or even wanted to quit. But you kept going. You practiced. And over time, your skill grew and so did your belief in yourself.

Confidence works the same way.

Perfection thinking tells you that you have to get it right before you begin. It says you can't mess up, look awkward, or need help. That kind of pressure shuts people down. It creates fear and hesitation. You wait until you "feel ready." But readiness doesn't come from waiting. It comes from doing. Overcoming this mindset is a crucial step in building confidence.

Confidence grows when you're willing to be seen trying not just succeeding.

Every time you speak up, even with shaky hands, you're practicing confidence. Every time you try again after something didn't go well, you're practicing. Every time you choose to keep going instead of giving up, you're practicing.

And yes, sometimes you'll make mistakes. Sometimes you'll feel embarrassed. But remember, that's normal. It doesn't mean you failed. It means you're learning. And confidence isn't about never falling it's about knowing you can get back up.

One of the biggest myths about confidence is that you need to feel brave before you act. However, it's often the action that brings the feeling. You take the step, and then the belief begins to take hold. That's why it's so important to stop waiting for the perfect moment. The moment is now. The confidence comes later. So, let's take that step together, right now.

The good news is that practice doesn't need to be big or dramatic. In fact, it's usually quiet and simple. It looks like:

- Saying what you really think, even if your voice shakes.

- Choosing rest when you're tired, instead of pushing past your limits.
- Asking a question, even if you're worried, is obvious.
- Saying no when something doesn't feel right.
- Taking a breath before reacting.
- Showing up, again and again, even when it's uncomfortable.

These actions don't look flashy. Most people won't even notice. But you will. You'll feel the shift. You'll feel your confidence strengthening, one moment at a time.

The more you practice, the more you'll trust yourself. Not because everything goes perfectly but because you've proven to yourself that you can handle what comes. That trust is what real confidence is made of.

So what gets in the way of that practice? A few things:

- Perfectionism. The belief that you must get everything "right" the first time or it doesn't count.
- Comparison. Looking at someone else's chapter 20 and assuming you're behind just because you're on chapter 3.
- Fear of judgment. Worrying that people will notice your effort and think it's awkward or not good enough.
- Impatience. Wanting results right away and giving up when they don't come fast.

But here's the truth: every confident person you admire started somewhere. They had awkward beginnings. They failed. They got things wrong. They didn't feel confident all the time. They just kept practicing. They kept showing up, even when it was hard.

You get to do the same.

It's also helpful to remember that progress in confidence isn't always linear. Some days, you'll feel stronger than others. Some situations will be easier to handle, and others will still challenge you. That's okay. Confidence is a living thing it grows, shifts, and responds to how you treat it.

Some days your practice might be bold and loud. Other days, it might be quiet and small. Both kinds count. What matters is that you don't give up on yourself when you don't feel perfect.

Try this: think of confidence like a muscle. You can't build strength by thinking about lifting weights. You have to actually pick them up. And you don't start with the heaviest one you start with what you can lift now. Over time, you build up more power. Not through magic. Through practice.

Confidence is the same. You don't become strong by waiting. You become strong by practicing.

If you need a place to start, try picking one small thing each day that stretches you a little:

- Speak up when you'd usually stay quiet.
- Try something new, even if it's messy.
- Give yourself credit for something you did well.
- Rest without guilt when you're tired.
- Ask for help, even if it's uncomfortable.

Each of those is a small practice. And those practices add up. They teach your brain: "I can handle this." They teach your nervous system: "It's okay to show up and be seen." And little by little, that becomes your new normal.

There's no finish line to confidence. You won't reach a day when you're done. And that's not a failure it's freedom. It means you're always allowed to keep growing, learning, and showing up without pressure to be perfect.

It means that even if today is hard, you can try again tomorrow.

You can build confidence your way. You don't have to copy someone else. You don't have to fake it. You just have to keep practicing in a way that feels honest to you.

Because practice is the path. Not perfection. Remember, every small action you take, every time you show up, you're building your confidence. And that's what it's all about.

Daily Thought:

"Confidence is something I build, not something I wait for."

Small Practice for Today:

Think of one situation where you've been waiting to feel confident before acting. Perhaps it's speaking up, starting something new, or being more authentic. Write it down. Now write one tiny step you could take today even if you still feel nervous. Do that one small thing. That's your practice.

Final Reminder:

Confidence is not about getting it all right. It's about not giving up when things go wrong. It's about showing up, trying again, and learning to trust yourself, even when it's uncomfortable. Perfection isn't the goal. Presence is. Practice is. Progress is. You're already doing the work.

Keep going.

DAY 28: COLLECTING YOUR WINS AS EVIDENCE

By now, you've probably done more than you realize. Over the past few weeks, you've noticed your thoughts, shifted your words, changed how you show up, and practiced confidence in real life. Even if it didn't feel perfect or even successful every time, you've still made progress. And that progress matters. Today is about something simple but powerful: collecting your wins.

Most people are good at remembering what went wrong. We replay our mistakes, hold onto embarrassing moments, and list our flaws with ease. But we rarely take time to remember what we've done right. We brush off compliments, forget how far we've come, and act like our wins don't count unless they're huge or public.

However, here's the truth: your brain requires evidence to accept new information. If you're trying to build confidence, it helps to show yourself proof that you're already growing. You need reminders that you've done hard things, made brave choices, and kept going. That's what collecting your wins does. It gives your brain real examples of your strength.

Confidence doesn't grow from being perfect. It grows from noticing when you try, when you show up, when you get back up after falling down. But if you're not paying attention, you might miss those moments. You might tell yourself the old story that you haven't done enough, or that you're still behind. That's why this practice matters so much.

So what counts as a win? Everything. Every choice you've made to support yourself. Every time you notice a self-critical thought, don't let it take over. Every moment you spoke up, rested when you needed to, asked for something you usually wouldn't, or simply stayed present instead of hiding. Wins don't have to be dramatic to be important.

Here are a few examples of small but powerful wins:

- You said "no" without apologizing.
- You reached out to a friend instead of isolating.
- You noticed a negative thought and chose not to believe it.
- You wore something you liked without worrying what others would think.
- You shared your opinion even if your voice shook.
- You made a mistake and didn't let it define your day.
- You rested instead of pushing yourself past your limits.
- You tried something new even though it scared you.

These may seem small on the outside, but inside, they are building blocks. Each one reinforces the belief that you can trust yourself. That you can take up space. That your needs and ideas matter.

It's easy to forget these moments because life moves quickly, and we're trained to focus on what's next. But reflection is part of growth.

When you stop to gather your wins, you reinforce your progress. You show your mind a new story one where you're not just trying to be confident, but where you already are in the process of becoming someone stronger, more grounded, and more honest with yourself.

Try this: take a piece of paper or open a note on your phone. Write down five things you've done over the past few weeks that you're proud of. They don't have to be big. They just have to be true. If it felt like a stretch for you, it counts. If it made you pause or breathe deeper, it counts. If it brought you closer to being yourself, it counts.

Now write five more.

Sometimes, your wins won't be visible to others. No one might see the internal battles you've faced. No one might know how hard it was to speak up, or rest, or show up when you wanted to hide. But you know. And that's enough.

This practice helps remind you that your work is real. That your effort is worth something. That you are allowed to feel proud without needing anyone else to validate it.

It also helps quiet the voice that says, "You're not doing enough." When you have proof in front of you, that voice has less power. You can say, "Actually, I am doing enough. I've done plenty. Here's the list."

You can repeat this practice anytime. Once a week. At the end of each month. Every time you finish something that stretched you. Keeping a "confidence file" where you collect these wins can become a quiet form of support a space you return to when doubt creeps in. On days when your confidence feels shaky, open that file and remind yourself: I've done hard things. I've grown. I'm not starting from scratch. I've already come far.

This kind of list also helps you define confidence in your own terms. You stop measuring your worth by how loud or bold or perfect you appear. Instead, you define it by how honestly you show up. How gently you speak to yourself. How often do you try again?

You begin to believe that your progress is real. And when you believe that, your next step feels less scary. You already have a track record. You already know you can keep going.

Here are a few journal prompts to support this practice:

- What did I do this month that took courage?
- When did I surprise myself by showing up more honestly?
- What's one thing I handled better than I would have a year ago?
- What hard decision did I make that helped me grow?
- What's something small I'm proud of even if no one else noticed?

Write your answers. Don't edit them. Don't downplay them. Just be honest. Let yourself name the wins that matter to *you*. This is your proof. Your personal list of confidence-building choices. It belongs to you.

And if you're struggling to come up with answers, pause and think again. Look for the small stuff. Did you keep a promise to yourself? Did you rest instead of overworking? Did you take a deep breath when you wanted to panic? Those are wins. Keep looking. You've done more than you think.

Today's practice is not about pushing yourself harder. It's about slowing down long enough to notice what's already working. It's about gathering the quiet proof that confidence is growing inside you, even if it doesn't always feel obvious.

Confidence isn't just a feeling. It's a pattern. It's the result of your actions, your choices, and your self-awareness. It doesn't come all at once. It comes through showing up, keeping track, and reminding yourself that you are already more capable than you used to believe.

And now, you have the evidence to prove it.

Daily Reminder:

"I don't need to be perfect to be proud. Every small step I take is a win worth remembering."

Today's Practice:

Make a list of at least 10 wins from the past month. Big or small, internal or external. Every one of them counts. Read them back to yourself slowly. Let them sink in. Let them remind you: this confidence is real. This work is working. Keep collecting the evidence you're building something solid.

DAY 29: YOU DON'T NEED PERMISSION TO BE WORTHY

FOR MOST OF YOUR LIFE, you may have looked outward for permission. Permission to speak. To try. To rest. To be proud. To feel good about yourself. It's something many of us are taught without anyone saying it directly. We're raised to wait. Wait until someone gives us a compliment to feel valuable. Wait until someone else says we're doing a good job. Wait until the room feels safe before we speak. Wait until someone tells us it's okay to take up space.

But worth doesn't work like that. You don't earn it by waiting. You don't need someone else to give it to you. You don't need permission to be worthy. You already are.

Today is about letting that truth settle in deep in your body, not just in your head. It's about realizing that confidence doesn't begin when someone else tells you you're allowed to be confident. It starts when *you* decide you are enough, right now, without needing to prove anything.

This can feel like a huge shift, especially if you've spent most of your life trying to live up to other people's expectations. Maybe you worked hard to be the "good one," the "strong one," the "smart one," or the "quiet one." Maybe you adjusted who you were to be accepted. Perhaps you've learned to ask, "Is this okay?" before sharing your ideas, voice, or genuine feelings with others.

There's nothing wrong with wanting to belong. We all want to be accepted it's a natural human desire. But at some point, many of us confuse acceptance with permission. And when that happens, we begin to believe our worth depends on how others react to us. We let their comfort become more important than our truth. We learn to shrink, not because we're weak, but because we think it's safer.

But the truth is: waiting for someone to "let you" feel worthy will keep you stuck forever. No one can give you permission to feel enough. That's something only *you* can decide.

You don't need to be more accomplished, more polished, more popular, or more prepared. You don't need a certain job, relationship, or appearance. You don't need to be the loudest voice in the room. You just need to believe that who you are, as you are, has value.

This doesn't mean you stop growing. It means you grow from a place of self-respect, not self-rejection. It means you're not trying to earn worthiness through perfection or performance. You're living from the belief that your worth was never in question to begin with.

Let's talk about what this looks like in real life.

It means raising your hand before you're sure your idea is perfect.

It means saying no, even if someone doesn't understand your reason.

It means resting without guilt.

It means saying what you feel without watering it down.

It means wearing what feels like you even if someone doesn't like it.

It means letting yourself be proud of what you've done, without waiting for applause.

It means not letting criticism shake your belief that you matter.

These aren't huge, dramatic acts. They're small daily choices. But each time you choose yourself, you reinforce the truth that your worth doesn't depend on outside approval.

If you've been taught that your value is something to earn, this shift can feel uncomfortable. You might worry that believing in yourself will make you selfish, lazy, or careless. But the opposite is true. People who know their worth tend to be more grounded, more generous, and more honest because they're not constantly chasing validation.

They're not proving. They're simply being.

So, how do you start living as if you don't need permission to be worthy?

You begin by noticing the places where you're still waiting.

Maybe you wait to post something until you're sure it will be liked.

You could wait to speak until someone else nods first.

Maybe you wait to feel proud until someone praises you.

Maybe you wait to rest until you've "earned it."

Start there. Notice the pattern. Then challenge it. Ask yourself: "What if I didn't wait? What if I believed I was enough already?"

This isn't about ignoring feedback or acting like you don't care. It's about knowing your foundation. When you believe you're worthy, feedback doesn't destroy you. It helps you grow. You can take it in without crumbling. You can hold your center even while learning.

Today's practice is simple. Write down the sentence: *I do not need permission to be worthy*. Then write it again. And again. Say it out loud if you can. Let it feel awkward. Let it feel bold. Let it feel like something you're not quite sure you believe yet. That's okay.

You're not trying to convince yourself all at once. You're planting a new belief. And the more you repeat it, the more it begins to feel real.

Confidence is not the absence of doubt. It's the presence of worth. And that worth isn't something you perform your way into. It's already yours. You don't have to earn it. You don't have to fight for it. You don't have to wait for someone else to say it's okay.

You just have to stop pretending it's not there.

What would shift in your life if you lived like that were true?

Would you stop apologizing so much?

Would you say no more clearly?

Would you rest more deeply?

Would you take a risk that matters to you?

Would you finally put something into the world that you've been holding back?

You are allowed to do all of these things. Not because someone gave you permission, but because you gave it to yourself.

So today, take one small step in the direction of that truth. One action that says, "I don't need to earn this. I already am enough."

Let that be how you walk into your day. Let that be how you talk to yourself. Let that be how you decide what you're willing to accept and what you're ready to let go of.

Because confidence built on someone else's approval is always shaky. But confidence built on your own self-respect? That's the kind that lasts.

Daily Reminder:

I don't need permission to take up space. I am worthy, always.

Today's Practice:

Write down three areas in your life where you've been waiting for approval. Now, for each one, write what you would do if you truly believed you were already enough. No more waiting. Just one small move toward living like you matter because you do.

DAY 30: BECOMING WHO YOU ALREADY ARE

You've reached Day 30. Perhaps that feels like a significant development, or perhaps it doesn't yet. But let's stop and look at what this means. You've spent thirty days facing thoughts that used to hold you back. You've questioned the lies you've told yourself, softened the voice of doubt, and tried things that may have felt uncomfortable. Even if you didn't do it perfectly, even if you missed some days or had moments where you slipped back into old patterns you're here. You kept going. And that matters more than anything else.

This final day isn't about becoming someone entirely new. It's about returning to who you've always been underneath the fear, the pressure, the roles you've played, and the stories you've been told. Confidence doesn't make you into someone else. It brings you back to yourself the version of you that was there all along, before the world convinced you to shrink, to stay quiet, or to wait your turn.

So much of personal growth is not about changing into someone better. It's about remembering. Unlearning. Coming home to your voice, your truth, your presence. The real you isn't hidden in some future version that has everything figured out. The real you is the one who tried. The one who got back up. The one who dared to say, "This matters to me." That's who you are.

When people talk about confidence, they often think of it as a final state. Something you achieve once you've done enough, earned enough, or fixed enough about yourself. However, the truth is that confidence is not a finish line. It's a daily choice to show up, even when it's hard. It's the quiet, steady belief that your worth isn't up for debate. It's a mindset, a practice, and a way of treating yourself with more care than criticism.

Over the last thirty days, you've made space for that belief to grow. You've learned that confidence doesn't have to be loud or flashy. Sometimes, it's the decision to keep showing up even when your voice shakes. Sometimes, it's letting yourself rest without guilt. Sometimes, it's saying no and not explaining why. And sometimes, it's standing in front of the mirror and not tearing yourself apart.

Confidence isn't something you wait for. It's something you build moment by moment, boundary by boundary, and word by word. And every time you spoke to yourself with honesty instead of judgment, every time you noticed an old thought and chose a different one, every time you said, "This is enough for today," you were building it.

The hardest part of this work is often giving yourself permission to be fully human. That includes the messy parts, the uncertain parts, and the parts that are still learning. Confidence doesn't require perfection it requires presence. And you've been practicing presence with yourself every time you've chosen truth over fear, progress over perfection, and courage over comfort.

So, what happens now?

Now, you keep going. You don't need to start over. You don't need to push harder. You simply continue. One small decision at a time. One thoughtful conversation with yourself at a time. One reminder, written in your notebook or whispered before you walk into the room: "I am allowed to be here. I am enough as I am."

You're not waiting for someone else to tell you you've done enough or that you deserve to feel good. You've already done more than enough. You've stopped the automatic habits of self-doubt long enough to notice them. You've created space for something new. And even if your mind still throws up old doubts now and then, that doesn't mean you've failed. It means you're still human.

Old thoughts may still show up. But now, you know how to respond. You've practiced noticing, pausing, and choosing differently. You've learned how to say, "That's not mine," and return to your own truth. You've learned how to stand your ground in small ways. You've learned how to speak with more clarity and care. And you've learned how to stop shrinking.

You've also learned that confidence isn't about being perfect it's about being real. It's not about never feeling scared it's about doing the thing anyway. It's not about always knowing what to say, it's about trusting yourself to speak when it matters. It's about walking into spaces like you belong, not because someone said you could, but because you've stopped asking for permission.

This is what becoming who you already are looks like. It's not a dramatic makeover. It's a steady, honest process of showing up more and more like yourself. Not a watered-down version. Not a performance. Just the real you.

You may still have moments of doubt. That's okay. Doubt is normal. But you've changed your relationship with it. Now, instead of letting doubt decide what you're allowed to do, you recognize it for what it is: a voice that used to protect you, but no longer needs to lead.

And now, you're leading yourself.

Today is your final daily lesson, but it's also your starting point. A beginning that doesn't require you to be anyone else. You're not missing anything. You don't need to be more polished, more liked, or more impressive. You're already whole.

So how do you carry this forward?

Keep choosing awareness. Keep speaking to yourself with kindness. Keep saying no when something doesn't feel right. Keep showing up even when it's uncomfortable. Keep practicing, not for perfection, but because you're worth the effort.

And most of all, keep trusting that becoming yourself fully is the bravest thing you can do.

Today's reflection is simple:

"What part of myself am I ready to stop hiding?"

Write about it. Think about it. Speak it aloud if you're ready. Let this be the start of a deeper honesty with yourself. Because the world doesn't need a more perfect version of you. It needs the real one. The one you've been slowly uncovering over the last thirty days. The one who knows that worth isn't earned, and confidence isn't something you have to wait for.

You are already everything you need to be. You just have to keep choosing it.

Daily Reminder:

I am not becoming someone else. I am becoming more of who I already am.

Today's Practice:

Write a letter to yourself from the version of you who knows you are already enough. Let it be a reminder you can return to anytime you forget. Keep it somewhere you can see it. Read it when you doubt. Believe it even before it feels fully true. Then take one step, however small, from that place of quiet knowing. That's what real confidence looks like.

30 DAYS OF CONFIDENCE JOURNAL PROMPTS

CONFIDENCE ISN'T something you have to be born with it's something you can build. One page at a time. One honest thought at a time. These 30 daily prompts are designed to help you think more clearly, speak more kindly to yourself, and show up more fully in your everyday life.

You don't need perfect answers. You just need a quiet moment, a pen, and a willingness to be honest. Some prompts will feel easy. Others might feel uncomfortable. That's okay. Growth doesn't come from doing it "right" it comes from doing it anyway.

This space is yours. There's no grade, no performance, no right way to respond. Just your real thoughts, your real words, and a growing sense of trust in yourself.

Come as you are. Leave a little stronger each day.

Day 1:

What does confidence mean to me right now? How does it feel in my body when I imagine having it?

. . .

DAY 2:

What's one message I grew up hearing that made me doubt myself? Do I still believe it today?

DAY 3:

Whose voice do I sometimes confuse with my own? How can I tell the difference?

DAY 4:

Where in my life have I been waiting for things to be "perfect" before starting?

DAY 5:

What's one thing I haven't done because I was afraid of being judged?

DAY 6:

In what ways have I been playing small? What would it feel like to stop?

DAY 7:

What does self-respect mean to me? How can I practice it more today?

. . .

DAY 8:

What is one thing my inner voice says that helps me feel strong? Can I write it somewhere I'll see it often?

DAY 9:

How do I usually speak to myself when I make a mistake? What could I say instead?

DAY 10:

What would it look like to speak to myself the same way I would speak to a close friend?

DAY 11:

When have I trusted myself recently? How did it turn out?

DAY 12:

What's one "I can't" thought I've had this week and what's a more honest version of it?

DAY 13:

When have I told myself I was "too much" or "not enough"? What's the real story?

. . .

DAY 14:

What does quiet strength look like for me? How can I practice it today?

DAY 15:

What's one thing I've been holding back from saying? How can I say it with honesty and care?

DAY 16:

What's one bold thing I want to ask for even if it scares me?

DAY 17:

When was the last time I stood up for myself, even in a small way? What helped me do it?

DAY 18:

How does it feel in my body when I speak clearly and slowly? What changes when I do?

DAY 19:

What thoughts come up when I walk into a new space? What would change if I walked in like I belonged?

DAY 20:

What does saying "no" mean to me? When is it hardest to say, and how can I practice it with care?

DAY 21:

When do I apologize too much? What could I say instead that still feels kind?

DAY 22:

What part of me tries to impress others? What part of me already knows I'm enough?

DAY 23:

What does safety mean to me now not from hiding, but from being real?

DAY 24:

When was the last time I didn't know something and felt embarrassed? How can I make space for "I don't know yet"?

DAY 25:

What is one promise I've made to myself but haven't kept? Can I recommit to it today?

DAY 26:

How do I act when I want to look confident? How does that compare to how I feel when I actually am confident?

DAY 27:

What would it look like to treat confidence as a practice, not a destination?

DAY 28:

What are five small wins I've had this month that I haven't fully celebrated?

DAY 29:

Where in my life am I still waiting for permission? What would I do if I already believed I was worthy?

DAY 30:

Who am I when I stop doubting myself? Describe that version of you in detail and how you can let them lead today.

IF YOU'VE MADE it to the end of these prompts, pause and give yourself credit. Writing things down especially when they're hard to say out loud is an act of strength. Even small reflections add up to big shifts.

Maybe your handwriting was messy. Maybe you skipped a few days. That's not failure it's real life. What matters is that you kept coming back. You made space for your voice. You showed up for yourself.

Keep these pages close. Revisit them when doubt creeps in. Let them remind you of who you are and how far you've come.

Confidence isn't about being fearless it's about being real. And you've done exactly that.

15 QUICK SCRIPTS FOR BOUNDARIES, ASKING, AND SPEAKING UP

Speaking up can feel uncomfortable especially when you're not used to it. Whether you're setting a boundary, asking for what you need, or saying how you really feel, it's easy to freeze up or second-guess your words. That's where these scripts come in.

Think of them as starting points, not rules. Each one is short, simple, and designed to help you practice direct, respectful communication. You can adjust the words to sound more like you. What matters most is the message: your voice matters, your needs are valid, and you're allowed to speak up without guilt or apology.

The more you use your voice, the easier it becomes. These scripts are here to help you take that next small, confident step.

Boundaries: Saying No Without Guilt

1. "Thanks for thinking of me, but I can't take that on right now."
2. "I'm at capacity, so I have to pass."

3. "That doesn't work for me."
4. Sometimes the simplest answer is the clearest.
5. "I need to leave this conversation for now. We can revisit it later if needed."
6. "I'm not available for that, but I hope it goes well."

Asking For What You Need

1. "I'd appreciate your help with this do you have time this week?"
2. "I need some space to think. Can we pause and talk later?"
3. "Could you speak to me about that more privately next time?"
4. "It's important to me that we both feel heard. Can we slow this down?"
5. "Can you explain that a different way? I want to make sure I understand."

Speaking Up: Honesty With Care

1. "I see it differently, and I'd like to share my perspective."
2. "I'm uncomfortable with how that was said."
3. Sets a clear tone without needing a long explanation.
4. "That doesn't feel respectful. Can we shift how we're speaking to each other?"
5. "I'm still figuring this out, but I want to say it out loud anyway."
6. A great script for practicing confident honesty even in uncertainty.
7. "I want to be honest with you, even if it's awkward. This matters to me."

Saying what you mean doesn't require you to be loud or perfect. It just asks you to be honest and clear.

If you've ever struggled to find the right words, that's normal. These scripts are here to support you, not to pressure you. With time and practice, you'll find your own way to say what matters and you'll do it with more ease and less fear.

Your words don't have to be fancy. They just have to be true.

Keep speaking. Keep showing up. You're doing better than you think.

CLOSING REFLECTION: KEEP BUILDING, KEEP SHOWING UP

CONFIDENCE ISN'T A FINISH LINE. It's not something you arrive at once and never have to work on again. It's more like a muscle something you build through repeated action, small choices, and the way you keep showing up for yourself day after day.

You've made it through 30 days of reflection, practice, and truth-telling. That's something to be proud of. But more importantly, it's a reminder that you don't need to wait to feel "ready" before you act. You've already proven that you're capable of choosing progress over perfection and self-respect over self-doubt.

Some days felt easier than others. Maybe there were moments when you didn't feel strong, or when the old thoughts crept back in. That's okay. What matters most is that you kept going. You stayed with yourself. That's real confidence not pretending to have it all together, but choosing to show up anyway.

There will still be times when doubt shows up. That's not failure it's just your brain trying to keep you safe. But now, you know what to do with those thoughts. You've learned how to pause, question, reframe, and respond with more truth and less fear. You've practiced what it means to speak clearly, stand tall, and ask for what you need not because it's always comfortable, but because you've decided you're worth it.

Confidence doesn't come from being loud. It doesn't come from perfection or comparison or approval. It comes from the quiet decision to trust yourself. To back yourself. To walk into the room like you belong even if no one else claps.

And if you ever feel like you're slipping back into old patterns, you don't have to start over from scratch. You just return to what you've already learned. You pause. You breathe. You remember: you've done hard things before. You can do this too.

So let this be your reminder: Keep building. Keep choosing small actions that feel honest and brave. Keep practicing boundaries, asking boldly, and telling the truth about who you are. And most of all, keep showing up not to impress anyone else, but to stay connected to yourself.

Confidence isn't a fixed state. It's a relationship you build with your own voice, your own worth, and your own ability to try again. Every time you speak with clarity, take up space, or say no when you need to you're reinforcing that relationship. You're reminding yourself: "I matter. My voice matters. I don't have to shrink."

This isn't the end. It's just another beginning. You've already started becoming the version of you who knows how to stand tall and stay rooted even when it's hard.

Keep going. You're already doing it.

Next in the Series

Love begins with the way you see yourself.

Love Mindset in 30 Days is a practical daily guide to healing old wounds, building self-respect, and attracting relationships that feel supportive and true. Whether you've been carrying past hurt, struggling with boundaries, or seeking to strengthen your approach to love, this book offers 30 days of precise, practical shifts to help you reset.

Each day includes a short reading, reflection, and practice to help you feel steadier, more open, and more grounded in love.

In just 30 days, you can start building a love mindset that begins with you and extends to every aspect of your life, paving the way for personal growth and transformation.

oshunpublications.com/imani-blake/love-mindset-in-30-days

BIBLIOGRAPHY

Anderson, A. (2019). The confidence code: The science and art of self-assurance What women should know. Harper Business.

Brené Brown, (2015). Rising strong: How the ability to reset transforms the way we live, love, parent, and lead. Spiegel & Grau.

Covey, S. R. (1989). The 7 habits of highly effective people: Powerful lessons in personal change. Free Press.

Dweck, C. S. (2006). Mindset: The new psychology of success. Random House.

Grant, A. (2021). Think again: The power of knowing what you don't know. Viking.

Heath, C., & Heath, D. (2010). Switch: How to change things when change is hard. Broadway Books.

Hoxsey, J. L. (2006). The magic of thinking big. Pocket Books.

James, W. (1890). The principles of psychology. Henry Holt and Company.

Kaur, A. (2019). Building confidence: The art of gaining self-assurance. Harper-Collins.

Kauffman, C. (2021). The self-love experiment: 15 steps to give yourself the love you've always wanted. Hay House.

Kondo, M. (2014). The life-changing magic of tidying up: The Japanese art of decluttering and organizing. Ten Speed Press.

Langer, E. J. (1989). Mindfulness. Addison-Wesley.

Lerner, H. G. (2013). The dance of intimacy: A woman's guide to courageous acts of change in key relationships. Harper & Row.

Lieberman, M. D. (2013). Social: Why our brains are wired to connect. Crown Publishing.

McGonigal, K. (2015). The willpower instinct: How self-control works, why it matters, and what you can do to get more of it. Avery.

Miller, W. R., & Rollnick, S. (2013). Motivational interviewing: Helping people change. Guilford Press.

Neff, K. (2011). Self-compassion: The proven power of being kind to yourself. William Morrow.

Peters, J. (2021). Confidence is key: The 5 essential steps to personal development. Harper Business.

Pink, D. H. (2018). When: The scientific secrets of perfect timing. Riverhead Books.

Robbins, T. (1992). *Awaken the giant within: How to take immediate control of your mental, emotional, physical, and financial destiny*. Free Press.

Seligman, M. E. P. (1998). *Learned optimism: How to change your mind and your life*. Pocket Books.

Shafir, E. (2013). *Scarcity: Why having too little means so much*. Times Books.

Snyder, C. R., & Lopez, S. J. (2007). *Positive psychology: The scientific and practical explorations of human strengths*. Sage Publications.

Tracy, B. (2017). *No excuses!: The power of self-discipline*. TarcherPerigee.

Welch, C. (2020). *You are enough: A step-by-step guide to unlocking your potential and stepping into your greatness*. Health Communications Inc.

ABOUT THE AUTHOR

Imani Blake is a mindset coach, spiritual strategist, and author of the 30 *Days to Alignment* series, where personal growth meets practical manifestation. Known for her clear, empowering voice and no-nonsense guidance, Imani helps readers shift their energy, rewire old beliefs, and attract the abundance they deserve—without burnout or fluff.

With a background in financial wellness and holistic coaching, Imani blends spiritual wisdom with everyday tools that actually work. Her mission? To help women—especially Black women—feel powerful, financially free, and deeply connected to their own worth.

When she's not writing or hosting workshops, you'll find her journaling at sunrise, curating her vision board, or dancing in the kitchen to 90s R&B.